New Voices

New Voices

A Collection
of Recent Nigerian Poetry

Edited by
GMT EMEZUE

HANDEL
Library of African Writing

New Voices (A Collection of Recent Poetry from Nigeria)
Anthology and Introduction Copyright
First published 2003
Revised Edition 2008.

World-Wide Web:
 Handel Books ltd.
http://www.hbooknetworks.com
In association with Africa Research International:
http://www.africaresearch.org

Published by
The African Books Network
Handel Books Limited
6/9 Handel Avenue
AI EBS Nigeria WA
Email: handelbook@yahoo.co.uk

Marketing and Distribution in the U.S. UK,
Europe, N. America (US and Canada),
and Commonwealth countries outside Africa by

African Books Collective Ltd.
PO Box 721
Oxford OX1 9EN
UK
Email: orders@africanbookscollective.com

Front and Back Cover: © African Books Network
ISBN: 978-36034-5-0

A Handel Book Publication

CONTENTS

Preface to the First Edition

NEW Voices is an attempt to record some of the art of the new generation of Nigerian poets – a move that had begun in the early nineties when the call for poems appeared in some Nigerian dailies. What followed then was the overwhelming response of enthusiastic first writers from all over the country. Now, almost a decade and half later, the maturation of effort has expanded the literary frontiers of this collection with the emergence of some wholly new and other fairly known writings in the beggarly charted field of Nigerian poetry appreciation.

We have followed an arrangement distinguished from past attempts at demarcations along themes and convenient publication periods. Compartmentalizing the poems, usually for tertiary or high school academics, is not quite relevant to the objective we set out to achieve in this volume being to present a wide list of readable materials that will appeal to all audience from whatever academic levels and nationalities they may come. Thus what we have is an admix of poems of varied sentiments and ideas while keeping in mind the significant character of the poetry of the recent generation being lucidity of expression and energy of breath not so fully or overtly explored by other generations before them.

It is our hope that this effort will sooner or later herald the distinctive merger of a new kind of poetry given the vibrancy, richness and expressive power of modern Nigerian writing. But, for now, the compilation has been fluid enough to allow past and present currents of national and trans national history that rile the poets' artistic temperament. Conspicuously absent here are Chinweizu and Osundare, including other poets from as far as the seventies whose works marked the convergence of this new poetry but who belong in a category where the term 'younger poets' may not strictly apply. However, the choice of excluding some of these forerunners of our new heritage takes exception in the poems of Enekwe and Nwamuo which, although having also begun from the seventies, find a parallel with the younger generation especially in their militancy and resurgence of nationalist spirit. These qualities have necessitated their inclusion among the new voices of this generation but it is a matter of opinion.

Many would share the belief that the project of poetry anthologies ought to hold out a dynamic culture naturally woven with our way of life, and should explore the range of realities so vivaciously and so contemporaneously in tune with society's educational and developmental needs. The

Nigerian society being a developing one – and so urgently in need of redemption – a worthy enunciation of the art of this generation should prove of relevance by its similarly evolving currency. On such a promissory note, there is little doubt that *New Voices* will be so updated as to keep connoisseurs regularly on their toes.

GMT EMEZUE
Dept. of English, Ebonyi State University
Co-ordinator, IRCALC African Library Project
for Africa Research International

DEDICATION

For younger Nigerian poets

ACKNOWLEDGMENTS

Most of the poems appearing in this volume are previously unpublished original works of the poets. Some, however, have been taken from published volumes. These include the works of authors received with their permission or on their behalf by their publishers and/or associates: 'Scuba Diver' by Peter Onwudinjo in *Women of Biafra and other Poems* ©Peter Onwudinjo 2000, All rights reserved; 'A Land Of Freedom' by Ossie Onuora Enekwe in *Broken Pots* ©Ossie Onuora Enekwe 1977, All rights reserved; 'No Way For Heroes To Die' by Ossie Onuora Enekwe in *Broken Pots* ©Ossie Onuora Enekwe 1977, All rights reserved; 'The Second Reptile' by Chin Ce in *An African Eclipse and other Poems* ©Chin Ce 1992 All rights reserved; May 29 1999, by Chin Ce in *An African Eclipse and other Poems* ©Chin Ce 1992 All rights reserved; 'Poems' by Peter Onwudinjo in *Women of Biafra and other Poems* ©Peter Onwudinjo 2000. All rights reserved. 'Even After The Grave' by Ossie Onuora Enekwe in *Broken Pots*, ©Ossie Onuora Enekwe 1977, All rights reserved; 'We Thought It Was Oil but It was Blood' by Nnimo Bassey in *We Thought It Was Oil but It was Blood* ©Nnimo Bassey 2002, All rights reserved; 'When The Earth Bleeds' by Nnimo Bassey in *We Thought It Was Oil but It was Blood* ©Nnimo Bassey 2002, All rights reserved; 'Mammon Worship' by Onuora Ossie Enekwe in *Marching to Kilimanjaro* ©Onuora Ossie Enekwe 2005, All rights reserved; 'Dictatorship' by Onuora Ossie Enekwe in *Marching to Kilimanjaro* ©Onuora Ossie Enekwe 2005, All rights reserved; 'Solitude' by Onuora Ossie Enekwe in *Marching to Kilimanjaro* ©Onuora Ossie Enekwe 2005, All rights reserved; 'Song Of Creation' by Chris Nwamuo in *Lamentations* ©Chris Nwamuo 1992, All Rights reserved; 'Bat Echoes' by Joe Ushie in *Lambs at the Shrine* ©Joe Ushie 2005, All rights reserved; 'The Call' by Chin Ce in *Full Moon* ©Chin Ce 2000, All rights reserved; 'Fortieth Avenue' by Chin Ce in *Full Moon* ©Chin Ce 2000, All rights reserved; 'Black Angel' by Chris Nwamuo in *Lamentations* ©Chris Nwamuo 1992, All Rights reserved; 'Mother' by Chin Ce in *Full Moon* ©Chin Ce 2000, All rights reserved; 'Inspiration' by Chin Ce in *Full Moon* ©Chin Ce 2000, All rights reserved; 'Confusion' by Chris Nwamuo in *Lamentations* ©Chris Nwamuo 1992,

14

The Art of the Younger Poets

THE emergence of a younger school of poetry with distinguishing temperaments from the new Nigerian counterparts was a welcome development for Nigerian writing. In spite of the dogged inventiveness of these bards within the new tradition, critics had set off the usual comparisons between old and emerging tendencies. But if there was any artistic distinction in the newcomers from their contemporaries, the better promise was laid in the expressive power which lifts their presumptuous craft into what, a few decades now, might prove a more credible testimonial of the times.

Assertions: The Changing Paradigm

The younger poets speak from very deep convictions, not tongue-in-cheek, but boldly, clearly and with less ambiguity. This paradigm of poetic anchorage I have called the Assertions. As divergent as they come with their opinions on every aspect of life, they sound much like ideologues with whom the faithful may find a mutual and convivial association. Yet their purpose, as may be stated, is not so much again to highlight distractive and discordant tunes of ideological war songs and fervent politicking as to unify the diverse manners of expression or individual ways of assertion, the expression of the "I" in extension. Here, poetry is the focal point. Attitudes toward circumstances of the times mark interesting points of individuality; their faith is committed only to that imagination with which they fashion worlds on hills beyond the rising sun.

The younger Nigerian poets are able to achieve this psychic poise, where nothing can throw them off their course, or where doctrines are not worth the sacrifice of a busy schedule, all because of an inner calm. The poet must develop a personality sufficiently stable in the stress and strain he must inevitably meet. Of course, he is free to sing or be all that he has chosen. He may be the extremist whose whispers whip werewolves like wasps, or she may become the revolutionary demanding justice amidst squandered hopes, yet with a will that cannot be broken as easily as the beating inflicted on him for the sake of his unyielding quests. Yes. He (or She) may, as well, become the chronicler of yester-pillage by modern political brigands, or the recorder of the pitiful howling of fallen roofs.

All these assertions are germane to his conscious experience, because he has been, and still is, part of that society where pugilist overlords deal merciless blows on the people forcing the poet to cry out: 'What is the meaning of this aimless business?' He has witnessed the madness of this society where everyone fervently pleads to be saved from one and the other self.

So how does he feel?

Sometimes his voice roars from the bellies of dark jungles and the shackles of iron cabins to the four posts of existence, screaming blood, freedom and vengeance. His actions are dramatised successively in leaps and bounds devoid of hidden eloquence. Yet eloquent are his words; they represent some shining exemplar of virtue despite the virulent scourge of vice. He is the artiste making his own musical notes out of the word as surely as the critic must weave his own foray from out the same word. His own notes are vibrant, pulsating words; they are songs of freedom and innocence when all barriers are broken and experience is the single teacher of life's lessons in love and laughter.

This song of innocence is thus an assertion of the purity of the soul unbound, not obliterated in the yawning void where danger lurks ready to close its jaws on the wary trespasser. With maturity, innocence grows into knowledge, and with knowledge an increase in poetic sensitivity. He had assumed an identity to champion the cause of change against the stagnation of his times. He had imbibed the spirit of coordinated action, becoming the fury of his placid age, the courage of his gutless era, the rage of his storm-less sea. This motivating challenge to his generation is imbued with the ferocity that dissolves mountains. The secret of success lies in seeking avenues and ways through limitations not really imposed by nature but, more significantly, arranged to stir the current of awareness that would jolt us into self-becoming, self-confidence and self-assertion, as they concur.

Thus the impertinence of the younger generation of Nigerian poets is not ended at all. If anything it has widened in dimensions of contempt or sheer distrust for the prevailing status quo. For Marxist thought, it was a dialectical and historical materialist struggle. For the poet of the new generation, the struggle more significantly, more psychically, must reflect in the subordination of the base, for the higher, self.

Within this divide is contained the greed and materialism of both worlds. Often our anger is made to becloud these to give them a bent of dignity. So the business of greed that informs that scoundrel system that our national flag hides is equally comparable in scope of criminality – and deserving of interdiction – to, say, those energetic hands of our public servants who go to grab, cheaply, pay packets for work they never did. Both symptoms fuel the growing decadence of the age. Thus when these criminals come with pretended messages and promises of a better life in the name of politics, the poet can see through all the hype.

He helps us to wear our suit of armour against such onslaughts upon our intelligence when he adopts a mien full of contempt and scorn for the perpetrators of this crime. In the warped thinking of failed leaders, for example, success is measured against the heights of their sky scrapers and the impregnability of their fortresses and security zones. Beef them up with grenades, the poet mocks; hide the truth with scrapers that touch the clouds. The local military and civilian surrogates of the rapacious West are natural targets for poetic scorn. The people's response is not just out of righteous indignation, as they are often wont to phrase it, but comes in red hot spleen.

The poetic interdiction is against all those responsible for stifling the human essence. Humankind is both the pitiable victim and the cowardly aggressor. It does not matter if the one has grabbed the reins of power and amassed the political machinery for his personal benefit, or if the other is the frenetic armchair revolutionary scheming, and generally bidding his time. He may be a part of that faceless throng of a no-nonsense mob rallied for the heinous murder of probably another of his ilk rather unfortunate to be caught in the act. And when he has done his judgment with the tyre, he is there when they wear the ordure frost on faces that glimpse never the faded silhouette of modern opulence. He is also there struggling among the upward social class to reach the top, and he must also come down among the spectators absorbed in the throwing of fists at the crude antics of those on the other side pushing to the front. But is it not the irony of human nature that for all our plodding, nightfall overtakes us at dawn? It is all pettiness and vanity; it is all a wasted effort! they scream. But who dares hold the fire of the burning sun? Nature, unperturbed, stares with mockery at history's fallacies. And as the earth rolls on its own infallible course, it comes with tomorrow and other revelations – from that permanent impermanence of states and conditions that terrorises the fool and his ignorant men.

It not just history that bears out the wisdom of the poetic assertions and interdiction; it is our perception of it – our limited partisan perspectives that finally reduce us to both victim and villain. The bard who is true to himself wants to be neither. He may afford to indulge in bouts of depression as well as flights of fancies. The world to him is that stage in which the drama of the absurd is enacted. People belong to the passing show. His visage is therefore ever-changing: snarling, jeering, amused, mocking, and always the aloof observer. Sometimes he is the clown who mimics himself. Other times, and rather crudely though, he jeers at the ugly faces of pimple-clustered sheet of eczema coats on our faces. Curiously, like the loud and vulgar preacher on TV too, his visage seizes upon morals: he yells about aborted blood kicking in the flowing streamlets of gutters.

Some poems may sound high-pitched in calumny but deliberate caricature of rabid xenophobia and the ignorance that witnessed petty tyrants decree the death on poets, or of that order of racial and cultural supremacists – the plundering wolf-gang of a blundering world. How about the fate of two applicants, one a gaily, pretty pearl, the other, brain and degree. What is it that would motivate the rating of her gait and face as worth more than his brain and books in the thwarted markets of the private sector? Is it also the strange logic that entrenched the clause of 'state-of-origin' in national administration and, in some parts of this country, placed the Pakistani in the position of judge of which Nigerian face constituted a non-indigene? It is significant to our poetry that no political system (in addition to those who would masquerade as champions of human rights) will bother to take a serious look at these and other little but highly important issues of tribal existence under one nation. It is thus important in our themes to have the perpetuation of corruption and bribery in many corridors of national power.

When the poets dissect these absurdities, they are compelling to some form of action people complacent in their own malaise, nose turned like the he-goat's, inhaling from putrid social wastes that do not better their conditions. Because our professed love for one another, both as individuals and nationalities, is like the spider's for

21

the fly. The younger poets show they are never aloof towards these 'mini-minded' attitudes which, littering the streets like Nigeria's mountains of rubbish, constitute eyesores curiously passed for modernity and civilization. The irony lies in matching the permissiveness of modern society with ours. There are some comic dimensions about our prodigal nationhood just as some attempts at pidgin seek to achieve unequivocal 'grassroots' communication. We can unravel the political innuendoes and comprehend the subtle contempt the poets hold for the penchant of indirection in our local, state and federal governments' policies. And this is not a matter for cheap 'Onitsha-market' chap books alone. The task before us, in committing words and ideas to paper, can only be achieved by conscious artistic discipline, and it must be understood from that parameter. It does not even accept a second place situation.

Frontliners and Visionaries

Like soldiers at the frontline, the younger poets have chronicled the crumbling of such obnoxious systems as the apartheid regime of South Africa and the pristine capitalism of the emerging right wing elites. For apartheid, the resistance of its right-wing conservatives was but the lashing of a parasite whose fate, quicker than his puny struggles for survival, everyone had rather liked to be sealed for the greater good. Some poets here were writing in the dying days of that regime when momentum had long gathered in the direction of change sweeping through Africa and her Southern neighbours. To call them Frontliners here is in tribute to the spirit of African resistance in the face of imperial forces that threaten humanity's survival on the planet. The downtrodden may only suffer for some time but the spirit ripples underneath every fragment of human effort. Even so, their suppression is only a matter of imposition within the physical realm.

We posit that freedom is a much more ethereal force belonging only in the realms where the essence of life is hence identified with the universal source of all things. Thus seeking expression in the crude regions of matter, space and time, it is but the pale reflection of that essentially unstoppable divine character which will, and must, prevail despite the circumstances of tyranny under which it is made to battle. The flaming wing of the eagle is freedom sped by justice; and from the ashes and brickbats of the violence, we can hear the cry of our spirit, pursuing its will, inspiring the song of the victim. The younger poets have discarded the sordid evidence of diabolical tortures and genocide which are hallmarks of chauvinist Boer and African governments. How beautiful the cry of freedom then sounds in the poet's ears. He is the cornerstone, the gold dust, the star in the garden swinging to freedom when the gates must have been opened with triumphal songs. The frontline is the poetic passage of history. It is a song for the roofless, recording the evidence of years of deprivation where, for instance, people eke out a living in thick standing papers and wooden racks, clamouring for a solid shrine to gather their scattered, battered lives. This is the picture of the world's governing elites that have no housing policy for the people save for themselves, and acute is the pain of it. At the frontline, the poets record the mood of fighters. It is one of angst toward their leaders at the home front who had screamed thus at apartheid: 'End racial discrimination!' while denying their suffering people even the barest means of survival.

The frontline poets warn of consequences. There are consequences of our greed, they tell us, which often take entirely unpredictable dimensions. It is nature's vengeance on tyrants who have no place in the dawn when galleys would not exist and where crops grow on common hills and valleys. If this latter assertion is an indulgence in *poetopia*, we find in the poet's inner conviction a statement of human triumph which stands against the opposing tendency toward despondency where the heart wills but is yet manacled, and where finally desolation is total.

The younger poets are visionaries of that which keeps man brimming with inspiration to brave the hardy. Theirs is not from the idle religion of the fanatic mapping out large portions of geographic disaster for 'infidels' or 'unbelievers' of his doctrine. Their seeing is rather of the constant experience of life; they are the vigilant observers who have come to note the pattern in the overall course of human destiny, a pattern such as that even-handed justice that commends the poisoned chalice to the owner's lips, for instance – or that which excavates the ghosts of our secret crimes to stand face to face before us at the border of the unknown.

In this pattern is hidden the secret of African wisdom, of ancient riddles yet unanswered. They dare the brave and courageous to taste of it and swoon in the forest of thousand daemons where truth kernels abound. Needless to say it is a creative effort, not the cult-like ablution associated with some initiation in obscurant depths. When poets become artistes on the sketch board of life, their imagination lifts them above the world of mundane, of rigid rules and stereotypes, to that fluid and formless state where strokes and strokes can make impressions of joy and myriad possibilities.

This creative talent is like the tree whose fruits have ripened more bountifully with sublime joy. Sometimes it can be a haunting feeling captured in a quest, a light like a blazing fire, and the trail is lost when the mind balks at the immense possibilities that stand before it. It leaves that nostalgic feeling of something lost, exteriorised in our mutual parting of ways, as in a discovery, or a simple good night bidding to a loved one. The poet walks the narrow lonely road of the world and only he knows the dew of sorrow that haunts his inner being reflected in his exterior world of inter-personal relationships to which poetry aligns the vision. For one point, after all the regurgitations of mere intellectual knowledge of past masters at our own illuminated expense, we shall come to the point where we can rekindle the beam of true enlightenment. Will the redeeming hope expressed here supplant the boundless cruelty of despotic governments in the truest sense? When the lagging rope is burnt after the executioner's gun blast, what will be left of cruel laws, of gaols and human rights nailed on the cross of judicial travesties? Or, as some have asked, what comes out of goal gobbled when clouds overtake the sun to steal the beautiful reflections in the mirror of our world?

There have been visions of war, thousands of cries echoed, and freedom lost; dreams of toxic deaths, and of the frustrations of climbers of the social mountain moaning and fawning in that manner that is the bane of the African elite. Self-spoilt and pampered, he had followed the allure of his nimble-footed white friends made in the modern wake of history. Deceived, he is abandoned to his own wits, and alone, is unsure of himself. The idea of mountain climbers as a parable of an African dilemma re-echoes the indictment against blind leaderships and the popular herd syndrome of their followers. One who has come to envision this becomes like soul at the peak of consciousness moulding dreams far above the crowded streets below. Upon the heights the vision is sharp, acute and reaches even beyond the times. It is then the prayer of the poet that no limitations should fetter the imagination. In such contemplation, silence is the thread upon which the thoughts run to stir in him the current of awareness and understanding. Here we seem to be treading towards the mystical and profound, which lies not merely in the words that form the tool of verbal communion but in the flowering rhythm of inner meaning. The poet is in communication with his own eternity, so to speak, because the image is more ethereal, more permanent; it belongs in the realms where space and time collapse and the dreamer is ecstatic about the discovery of whatever he had sought.

Dreams are thus the living image in the centre of the eye. We long for that eye of eternity in which lies the power that lifts the veil over all secrets and lays bare the shoddy crimes in the chambers of mind. The song bird is let free, let to roam over the whole world of consciousness. The tongue of the bard is loosened likewise, free with the power of expression, because he is communicating an essence that touches the very core of being, reaching beyond words, mere symbols, beyond the body which belongs to the world of matter. The mysteries appear to fade, for no longer is he a child of the world staring with rose-coloured eyes and crawling behind time; rather he rises beyond space and time, and true knowledge is revealed, mysteries understood. The morrow is no longer bound with a thick fog for this is the product of the mind of space, matter and time. But listening into the shadows and taking the lonely route of realization, he discovers himself. Friends are gone, and what is left to do is to play the game of silence which hides the wisdom of his being. He learns that shadows don't hurt. Instead there is the discovery of what is in the word, the word that had sung the fame of great men and women and bubbled in minds tortured by social limitations. The word turns him restless and often drives him to strange deeds, such as committing suicide on a rope, shooting self in a hotel room, or making a pact with alcohol. It is clear then that he does not have any diplomatic (or artistic) immunity against the heat and cold, the comforts and wants of existence in the world. But if it is the outside world we know that he sings of, then there will always be hunger and war, hatred and evil. Because it is a world of greed and pride, of sadness and contentment, lust and vanity. It seems then a foolish attachment to a world of myriad illusions for man to think that he can amass every inconceivable possession and actually identify his being with these fleeting products of material fancy. His physical body may be heading to the grave but his amnesiac mind does not even want to contemplate this. Frantically he runs to the cosmetics and paraphernalia that sustain the illusion of physical prowess. But for the bard, death bound is home bound. Has he caught life's thread of continuity beyond so real to our ancestral lords and kin? Is that why he proclaims rest not in peace against that commonly touted yet meaningless pronouncements by graveyards? With such a visioning comes knowingness, like the seed, buried in the womb of the earth and blooming into life. As the poet I know this by going within that silence where nothing is lost but the fears and frustrations that tie the mind to the impermanent world, and I declare: the tunnel of death ends at the gate of life.

Love, Nature and Sweet Remembrances

Now how about the eternal subject of love that has baffled tyrants and amused sages for generations? The subject of love is the attempt to recover the gallant chivalry of poetry in a world reduced to a mere materialistic equation. Consider the child's reminiscence of that age of the cradle hands clasped around mother's, ear rested between her breasts evoking a tenderness perfect with mother and child. Or the boundless love of God for man as in the rhapsody: 'See! Your tears are in my bottle stored, and when you grieve and feel distraught, my love fails not to flow... .' Love is also the paternal exhortation to a new born baby, or the love of friends epitomised in those giggles of long-gone years ringing in the loving heart. It is the crown the mate of the goddess may wear when deepest yearnings are filled and reaching to heavenly heights. Nothing could ever hinder these reflections as does the poet by the lamp side. It renews the dream, it is the warmth in the night that the poet edifies in his love verses. Even the doctrine of sin can find a hope of remedy in this love, symbolised in the sun whose rays brighten the days of gloom. Yet love, the poet shows, can be a refuge for the hypocrite, his rationalisations and monumental deceits. This latter sense of disillusionment is part of the general paradox. Love is sought even in the dream of a soul mate where any affair, for the poet, becomes like truancy in infancy, no longer needed within the circle of perfect harmony that comes with graduation.

And love is ambiguous. Its ambiguity is of a kind built on language and mind. But it is one that may be transcended when all fears are pushed back and hope is allowed to assimilate the meaning of the message framed with care. The poets of these verses are, thankfully, seeking to lend verbal and auditory expressions to thoughts and visions that normally seem like idealism – proving that rabid materialism has not totally swept our generation away. To be regained here is the true sensitivity which, even when piteously quixotic in modern times, truly ennobles our lives. In seeking the well-being of others we imbibe the timeless virtue of loving care. So the young poet asks: What is as strong as love? rhetorically, for the unseen force that shapes lives and gives a few men the courage to do invincible deeds, heal unhealable wounds and cure incurable sores. It is the power beneath the swift's endless flight, and the graphic play of bowers in flight, and the dance of the lek birds so cooly, so unhurriedly. Love is the rare bird with bright colours. It is nature in motion, lost to mundane and artificial perceptions; but now recovered in the picturesque imagination of poetry, the scope and meaning is most unquantifiable in simplistic terms. Yet its persistence, despite its elusiveness in the circumstances that force us to part from our beloved, is transcended by hope and faith. To be fondled and admired forever, or to be given a name; to be free, depends upon the enduring hope and faith of love. Like the candle that kindles the light of knowledge, love illuminates all doubts and dark corners of the soul. It glows with excitement; it throws beautiful patterns on floors and walls. Its essence is like the water of life which flows to sustain life in every universe; and without it, what calamity, what hazards and disaster and doom would befall mankind; how could we face the world without it?

As in his love, the poet's sympathy to nature is a widening of the scope of poetic inspiration which is more than just Romanticism. Indeed this is, if anything, the age of materialism where every value is being eroded in the survivalism wrought by global preying on human and natural resources. But still the poet may fantasise on the moon or rain in a manner of imagination that cannot be interpreted within the theoretical stream. Even if his purpose is to experiment with word and sound, the splash and slash, the slushing and cascades, the rush and bubble and rumbling and babbling are creative attempts to translate the auditory and the visual into strong, almost palpable reality.

Let the rainbow be an inspiration of wonder hiding the secrets of ancient wisdom and the puzzle of positive, negative and neuter elements of the universe. Such too is the nature of the stars that their luminous smiles around the galaxies operate on realms beyond the ignorance of the seeing and blind. What other secrets lie behind this calm composure of an unfailing cycle of nature? What truths do nature and creation endow the heart that experiences its bliss? Our love for nature would ultimately lead us to that longing for the childlike state wherein beauty and the grace of intuition and joy, explicit joy, all become the temperament from which our emotional fabric may always be cut.

We can learn from the nightingale, singing the same tone as ever, a fidelity that even a preacher may never have. A consistency in the peace, love, and sweetness of nature is reflected in lunar tenderness and gracefulness. Thus it is not an act of ordinary emotion to ejaculate about nature so good, nature so kind. Rather it is an awakening to higher truth, recognising the infallibility of nature's order in all things. How close our perception, or how keen our perceptiveness, depends on our different levels of awareness. It can be as keen as the poet admiring the cyclic regeneration which permeates all life including the many countless wide ripples in nature and existence. This philosophical dimension of poetic perception suggests another look at the other end of the scale, the negative aspect of the rainbow which tends to fight the other side of nature so harmonious and peaceful. Indeed, there's two to life, as poets tell – even when they complement or seem to negate: the storm and the calm. The purpose, as may be seen, is to find a balance at the point where the poet calls the middle bearer.

Poetry is the eye of reminiscence, and a complex one too. The poet is involved in a kind of introspection, a communication with his own self and the extension of this self as reflected in others with whom he shares mutual experience. He may be reaching out into his box of memories as far back as a little incident of childhood, recalling the feelings, the mood of that singular moment in no mean feat with words. For those dramatic incidents of life, which jolt us out of complacency and leave a permanent imprint, like a scar, upon our subconscious mind, may appear incomparable in inner depth and significance with that subtle, very normal incidents that had been long overlooked but now unearthed in the mind's screen when looked upon with the eye of the moment. A fresh insight is gained, the lessons subtler and thrilling to discover; its discovery more than measures our present growth: point B against that previous stage of history: point A. It could open up a wider frontier of viewpoints for understanding of our own self, our experiences, our associations, our loves and hates. The spiritual realization that may accompany this experiencing is in every way limitless. What is that force that pulls strangers together in a definite place and bids them interact like old friends? Had they really met before in a distant time; is that parting a re-enactment of a some experience in the dim past and which must recur in some future with that timed mathematical ordering of the universe?

What is it that we harbour in our memory-bag of history? A life of distant years which remembrance may be triggered by the most casual events and actions as in the flight of a bird? A poet's land of red soil where homesteads clustered together and lizards moved in their pairs? Such a land of laughter, hunting and merriment often haunts us with its romantic symmetry. This re-experiencing of memory, these reminiscences, would unearth subtleties of emotional states when contrasted with harsh physical realities: anger at the rude awaking of a nation by idle military adventurers or indignation at the invasion of the peace of a continent and subsequent imposition of alien values on a people – that flagrant violation of personal spaces – in what has been called colonialism and, in religion, evangelism.

Memory is history, yet a more intense kind of history. Its re-experiencing focuses the attention and magnifies the feeling to the extent and degree of our focusing. Thus the pangs of SAP, that symbol of our economic slavery, had marked the time of dogs and registered the insipidity and lifelessness that trailed our poverty and corruption in its most monumental scale. In Nigeria, SAP was that promise unfulfilled, leaving the masses dying before the promised recovery of market laughter. SAP or SFEM: a negative inspiration for poetry. Its vaunted acronym was shown to be essentially depressing and the poet does not relent in pointing this out. Under SAP all remains of nationhood was sapped in oblivion, leaving a deep trail of cynicism and hopelessness. Lying and still running in the projector of the poet's mind are the skulls of souls silenced on the acrid journey to the altar of power. And like SAP, Koko came to symbolise the indolence of a nation under the illusion of its size and military strength which it foolishly turns on its own citizenry. Here was a nation caught napping when huge drums of toxic waste were being imported and dumped on its soil.[1] Issues of national significance did not pale with the reality of private experiences within which had lain the hope that the cries of yester years may fade far into the dying flames. The lost emerald of hope is regained at last. In fact within the personal world lies a stretch of possibilities – love and mutual giving of self, travel and adventure, meeting and parting, places distant, strange treeless lands and deserts, friendships made, cherished, and friendships lost after the parting.

The human truth in these experiences makes for their reality, the deeper significance appealing to the humanity within our universal essence. For instance, how does the poet succeed in evoking an ironic feeling of nostalgia in the poem of the 'been-to' living 'in a kind of quarters'? We can enjoy the soft rhyming of the lines and the philosophical contemplation which endows truth upon what may have been a mere subjective escapade.

Let us concede that life consists of these many journeys. Through the many different planets, continents and

---

[1] Not surprisingly the younger poets found very little to commend the military government of self-styled "President" Ibrahim B.abangida during the mid eighties and early nineties of his regime when these events happened.

worlds men and women have travelled, crossed many waters and bridges, traversed space and journeyed in time. Each experience leaves a definitive stamp, an image, and like a screen-sheet filled and stacked with them, they haunt us with their grim and grotesque distortions. Our recall of them comes in parts, and it comes to take the unconscious shapes of our own nature. It could be the smoking chimneys in the harmattan mist. Here the tool of perception is, as always, the poetic sensibility. The couch heading up North assumes a snaky steady strain mingling in the oratory of commercials and vistas of living greenery and parched yellow plumes. What brotherly flight of fancy links this rhythm to the Negro gospel? And what imagination metamorphoses the rocks of Jos plateau into bare backs of crouching giants, grim monarchs hunched in colloquium? We capture the hoary transport crisis in Lagos, and Onitsha creates a picture of people who build their powers on pillars of pain beating limitations to make their millions. The journey takes us to Abuja and to Umuahia where it evokes an invitation to a war that had been fought and ended: Umuahia, once the capital of Biafra, home town of Aguiyi-Ironsi, one of Nigeria's murdered leaders like Balewa and Mohammed before and after him. We traverse Lagos once again, the commercial nerve centre, Nigeria's New York and repository of a fearfully tumultuous traffic lagoon. The

37

image resonates in the pattering of raindrops in that crowded city. In our journey, thoughts are meteors, events comets which seem to take us to our destination even before the blink of an eye. Sometimes visualising can really become tactile. It is like transcending the limitations of the present and entering into that state which is visualised and finding inside it a reality that is irrefutable to the experience.

Here in this collection we are also witnesses to a few nursery poems. In the past it had appeared that the nursery was a less creative activity than the general themes that deal with social conditions. The question of profundity had tended to be exaggerated, so also the indulgence in obscure poetry. What concerns the poet of nursery is the peculiarity with which familiar themes are expressed, their general lucidity and lyricism. Nowhere are these qualities exemplified than in these poems where a pattern of repetitions and parallelism, very familiar in oral poetry, is experimented with striking effect. There is some a kind of entertainment in the rhetoric which, though simple, does not suggest naivete – the charge of chauvinists for the complex and mystical. Nor must rhyming be forced. Rather to flow without exaggeration or inducement is the candid deal. Consider the straight assertiveness of some lines of 'Going to School' and 'Gentle Birds.' In marking a little spot for the child audience, the editor has rightly considered that poetry can essentially assume the auditory medium of expression which can stimulate greater interest by the virtuous arrangement of verbal and other sound effects, and, at the same time, remain accessible to the sensitivity of the truly younger generation to leave a lasting legacy for the future times.

And so here, in the assertions of the younger poets, here, in the art of the new generation of Nigerian poets, we have become frontline men and women... and visionaries... and lovers of all that may be true of all ages, among all nations, all races, all cultures the world over. Here then lies the art of the younger poets.

CHIN CE

Recent
Nigerian
Poetry
(1990-2008)

CULTURE

Bass drums explode across the omelette
Mat melting over the sky.
VIPs stream past in storm motorcades
Oh, the monsoon bassoon of their sirens!
In a fell swoop the untarred motorways
Cast a blanket of dust over the entire
Gay troupes hemming their sidewalks.
Pieces from the garbage heaps trapeze;
Bushes clone the steps of gods;
Trees shake their hairy heads and beady waists -
Soon, when the durbar of dust
And discarded cans is done;
When high hearts have chinked;
Tom-toms, timpani, snare drums have rolled;
Soon, when sweat has gushed and
The pit stop is reached,
Soon… not a single green bead shall
Respond to all the might that might call.

AHMAD MAIWADA

LAGOS

Lagos welcomes you - the sagged
Ex-sweetheart, waving sweaty palms;
Swarming you with salty smiles
In unwashed teeth, charming you
Into the slaying squeeze
Of her sticky streets.

Should you submit, the ghouls snoring
In her grubby armpits will rise,
Like sphinxes to asphyxiate you.
Unsleeping, she will yawn,
Unlocking the tons of unchewed
Garbage in her mouth, as her
Constipated colons
Rumble with stolen hopes.

Today, brooms of rains
Search her rooms for her lusts,
Her rusts and rats that mate
In her corridors and dare
The watching moon tell his God.
Cleansing done, dark dung dribbles
Down her southern routes,
Like the curse, to plunge into
The yawning mouths of the sea.

AHMAD MAIWADA

IN THE BEGINNING

Back to the days of old
Bright- red guardian flames
Shimmering pride,
Beautiful to the eye
Sparkling
crystal reflections
Hot liquids of non-existence
Drying off below
And above,

In the beginning of things
In the likeness of its maker
We emerge to a world bestowed.

MICHAEL O'BROWNE

THE BRICK DISSOLVES IN THE CRYSTAL SEA

The brick dissolves in the crystal sea
The hour of life has come
Take your bow
Voice of a horn, of flutes, of drums and cymbals
Stride the ancient orchestra
You have inherited the word
Its flesh, its wine
It is bread, it is blood
What fire in our bones
Sad rivers, the infinite ache ...
The night is afflicted with arrows
The wind your companion is whispering
Greet the throne of sapphire with the
voice of centuries
You stroke a note rich in sun and song.

TOYIN ADEWALE

SCUBA DIVER

Poetry does not petal
on the reef of words
nor grows in shallow seas.
It blooms in the harts of clams
that cling to the depths
in the mind's plumbless sea.

A poet needs more than plunge and swim
the scuba diver's tanks, flaps and fins;
He needs an oiled tongue to sort
the tangled mass
jostling for rainbow colours
Hustling to break the surface
plucking new chords.

PETER ONWUDINJO

A LAND OF FREEDOM

He loved his people
and found for them
a new farm in the east.
They cheered:
  OSAGYEFO
and followed him.

The paths were full
of snakes and thorns,
and so, endlessly
in want of beds,
they called him a hawk
and murdered him.

OSSIE   ONUORA ENEKWE

RAIN SEASON

The time has come
when the tree will drink
from heaven's waters

and leaves bloom
with joyous evergreen

The time has come
when the farmers shall go
eagerly to the farms

to return with fruits
of many labours

The time has come
when quietly we shall sleep
and put behind-

ugly memories of dry seasons
with the glazing heat.

OKEY IFEACHOR

NO WAY FOR HEROES TO DIE

I sing to the memory of those who died to be forgotten—
carcass of heroism stung by rainbows,
stung till blanched, it was abandoned by flies,
femurs and joints juggled by the wind
foretelling the apocalypse of muscle-bound people.

I sing of Nzeogwu, Achibong and 'Atuegwu.
In the field, their scattered bones jeer
at the azure sky, and sneer at the masked terrors of
    rainbows.
Rain drops endow them with their colours
until they all dissolve in the perpetual moulding of the
    earth
where the worms that groan endlessly in the mud
tumble them through their guts
making a clamour within the crusts of eternity.

Some heroes are carved in stone for the blind to see.
Others disintegrate in the shifting seasons.
Nzeogwu died like a lamb ripped apart by invisible
claws,
his body drawn in the dust that could not rise enough
to tell his people of his whereabouts.
Achibong's head dropped when a coward found
heroism
in a hatchet chopping the neck. of a fallen soldier.
Atuegwu died in a dark cell while he waited for
prosecution.

Now, many years after, they are forgotten,
their bones lost in the desert of their fall,

their resolve turned into .folly
by hungry historians and starveling professors.

This is no way for heroes to die.

OSSIE   ONUORA ENEKWE

THE SECOND REPTILE

Scrapers line the sky
Haughty monuments
Flank the barracks of the new reptiles.

Beef up security with grenades
Around lonely reservations in distant
Dodan wilds
(After the jets had scorched the earth
Against the foes that lurked in demented
East)

Here, boy, swagger through te streets
In epaulettes
And silverstick
To take your gourd of honour –

And there, let your guards
Sweep the streets of snivelling verrmin.

Nigeria may pray forever while
His grave side must read the epitaph:
He built a nation of scrapers
To hide the truth from the sun.

CHIN CE

POEMS

In the sky of the mind
great poems are made;
First, plough the floating fecund clouds
then, seed them inspiration
and watch the seeds of mystery grow:
    On the wings of sprouted thought
    laden clouds cluster and sing
    and ride to earth
    in showers of verse
    fresh like the rains of May.

PETER ONWUDINJO

EVEN AFTER THE GRAVE

My generation passes away
like comets in the gloom.
Awful to watch them go!
Friends in dry and wet seasons,
foes of all that would torment me,
die like wax light in the storm.
In the city
there is one still bound to go,
who still loves me,
as if he never met any better,
who said to me
in the dark room
where he lies day and night:
"If I lose you,
I'll know I have
lost a friend."
His mother, face deep-furrowed
by gourds of hope on pain,
waits as double night threatens her son,
before young and fresh as sapling,
today, thin and fragile like reeds
when Harmattan has settled
to rule or ruin.
I care not for skulls
nor for aging bones,

broken cords and wrinkled skin.
I fear for us that build
this place for bloom
and see a high rockwall
between the dead and the living.
There is no fence,
no dead or living.
The dead are distant friends
who refuse to write or call.
Kevin lives, ready
to sketch his friend whose voice
he loves as much as the person;
Igboji rides his autobike
forward and back, and Utsu's
golden-gong voice
still tickles sad lips.
So even after Togo's death,
what cry does one utter,
but that of love?
There is love
even after the grave.

OSSIE   ONUORA ENEKWE

MAY 29 1999

A sluggard slouched
In his paunches
On to Aso Rock

To smear the palace walls
With his slovenly mirth.

Many gruelling months
We watched the lame duck
Wobble his elephant kite
Around the gang of wolves.

May 29 is kakistocracy day
He will make the klieg light
Of minds like his cracked
With the disease of road blindness.

What further curse of the
Triangle
Awaits your children, folks,
If you let them.

CHIN CE

WE THOUGHT IT WAS OIL... BUT IT WAS BLOOD
(To Oronto Douglas & youths of the Niger Delta)

The other day
We danced in the street
Joy in our hearts
We thought we were free
Three young folks fell to our right
Countless more fell to our left
Looking up,
Far from the crowd
We beheld
Red-hot guns
We thought it was oil
But it was blood
We thought it was oil
But it was blood
Heart jumping
Into our mouths
Floating on
Emotion's dry wells
We leapt in fury
Knowing it wasn't funny
Then we beheld
Bright red pools
We thought it was oil
But it was blood
We thought it was oil
But it was blood...

First it was the Ogonis
Today it is Ijaws
Who will be slain this next day?

We see open mouths
But hear no screams
Tears don't flow
When you are scarred
We stand in pools
Up to our knees

We thought it was oil
But it was blood

We thought it was oil
But this was blood
Dried tear bags
Polluted streams
Things are real
When found in dreams
We see their Shells
Behind military shields
Evil, horrible, gallows called oilrigs
Drilling our souls

We thought it was oil
But it was blood

The heavens are open

Above our heads
Toasted dreams in
In a scrambled sky
A million black holes
In a burnt sky
Their pipes may burst
But our dreams won't burst

We thought it was oil
But it was blood
We thought it was oil
But it was blood

They may kill all
But the blood will speak
They may gain all
But the soil will RISE
We may die
And yet stay alive
Placed on the slab
Slaughtered by the day
We are the living
Long sacrificed

We thought it was oil
But it was blood.

NNIMO BASSEY

OKITI'S INCANTATION

I am Okiti
The man ant hill,
Okiti, Akaraogun's child,
brain-drain unbeatable
The scheming snake under the grass yonder
The hiding grass- the serpent,
The blinding potent serpent
Unseen serpent under grass
If the grass not hide the serpent
Then hay grass will burn it
Let no man set ablaze the grass
Let no one stare Okiti in the face
Okiti,
The suicidal conqueror!

M. A. SADIQ

AKARAOGUN

I am Akaraogun
The poisonous cake,
If salted and eaten,
It kills
Swallowed it suffocates,
If smelt gaseous and dusted,
It blinds, paralyses,
If seen, ridiculous, mere muted,
It mars, destroys the senses.
I am the metallic lead arrowed canon,
Canon balls of no mean destruction,
The arrow maced, honoured progenitor,
The blinding thundering blaze,
That strikes from mountaintop
Of no man's sin can say.

I dare not miss,
Precision.
Aye!
I am!

M. A. SADIQ

61

OKITI'S ANSWER

When the cock crows
A lazy man snores
In the morning.
As the morning dawn
Hypnotises an indolent
Thus I, command you,
To sleep by
Wool bat and the broom!

M. A. SADIQ

WHEN THE EARTH BLEEDS

I hear that oil
      Makes things move
In reality check
      Oil makes life stop
      Because

The oil only flows
When the earth bleeds

A thousand explosions in the belly of the earth
      Bleeding rigs, bursting pipes
This oil flows
      From the earth's sickbed
      Because

The oil only flows
When the earth bleeds

They work in the dark
      We must lift up the light
Quench their gas flares
      Expose their greed
      Because

The oil only flows
When the earth bleeds

In conference halls
        We talk in gardens of stones
The ocean waves bathe our eyes
        But in Ogoniland we can't even breathe
        Because

The oil only flows
When the earth bleeds

What shall we do?
        What must we do?
Do we just sit?
        Wail and mope?
Arise people. Arise
        Let's unite
With our fists
        Let's bandage the earth
        Because

The oil only flows
When the earth bleeds

The oil only flows
When the earth bleeds

NNIMO BASSEY

SONG OF CREATION

Sprout....
everlasting green plant
in contact with mother earth.
From the purgatorial subjugation
of the ego
bloom a beautifully scented
wicked branch
giving the ignis rocks
a false wintry shelter
life is cotyledon lost
to immortal sand.
The give and take of creation
compel streams run through
to rocks of regeneration.
The Saviour's immortality
sings praises of abandonment
a beatific nature
at the watergates.
Play life's billiard
on the dry banks of Imo river;
the difference of seven and two
is obedience to the Song of Creation.

CHRIS   NWAMUO

LOST LOVE

When the weather is chilly
When the icy wind blows
And heaven's water gate is opened
I remember, painfully
I was yours
Though the time was short
It was a pleasant time, gay time
I opened my hands to clasp your love
But you had left me…

I wish we could continue
Forever being one
I love you so dearly
It's hard to describe
I'll never forget you
As long as I live.

OKEY IFEACHOR

KOKO

Our security watched towards the west
While we daily lay at rest;
With our land and sea on sight
Enemies kept out of our sight...

What, we thought, had we to fear
Our arms were shears, they could tear
Our towering figure readily tallies
With allies in all rallies

Our ports were secured,
None can be bothered
Our sentries alert
None would ever make a flirt.

Who could fly an alien in
When only air could filtrate in;
Only grains could move passports
So, see the strength of our fortes!

Our navy like was so brave
They would dance to any stave;
They admire all notes
Oh! our love for foreign notes.

Then health began to ail
As treacherous air prevailed
Our cause turned a sport
Koko is made a toxic port.

When hoariness attends our age,
We will relate all of that age
Were we always achieved nought
Save being sold when our thought
Dances at tunes from foreign notes.

DUNMADE IBUKUN

BAT ECHOES
(For Alade Richard Mammah)

Each dusk when the world retires to bed
the hanging pensive young bat counts his
curses and fires these endless queries:

What was my ancestors' offence against
the god of creation that he singled me out
as the only creature through whose one mouth
I must feed, vomit, excrete and procreate?

What was my ancestors' offence against
the god of creation that he singled me out
as the only creature that rests upside-down?

What was my ancestors' offence against
the god of creation that he singled me out as
the only creature whose identity bestrides the
rodents
for our shared teeth and the birds for our shared
wings?

From the homosapiens at dawn, the young
black's echoes of the young bat's queries
pierce the heart like a kiln-fired arrow:

From the streets of angel-less Los Angeles where
Rodney King's voice, hoarsed by batoning by those
keepers of the peace, rekindles that ungoing scar
on the world's forehead like eyeless Polyphemus;

From South Africa where the dust from the chasing
of that bare-footed black by the helmeted policeman
and his humanised alsatian dog is just settling;

From Lagos where life's vibrancy for the youth
is the vibration of traffic agonising his residence
beneath the overhead bridge crossing to alien
Alien Avenue, Victoria Island and Ikoyi;

From Somalia and Liberia where human ego
feasts on fresh human flesh felled by firing
and swells the vultures into belching balloons;

From Brazil where the young black's life has
dwindled like the value of third world currency,
where, like the violated Maori, the children
are murdered for a few as an honour;

From Central African Republic where
school children are minced meat in saucers
to brighten the glooming mood of the Emperor;

From the homosapiens at dawn
the young black echoes the young bat's queries:
How grave was my ancestor's offence against the gods
that wherever I am the grave stares me in the face?

JOE USHIE

THE CALL
(beyond the sun rising)

Because I have seen how long the road
Lies beyond the setting minds of men
Revolutions may rumble down the highway
There'll be confusion after the thunder

Because I looked past the hungers of today
And drank some deep beyond the doctrine
I can look the raving tyrant in the eye
And see the yawning emptiness of his glare

For gone is the wind from too many prophets
Who struggle for all of heaven's seats
Because I have heard the call of soul
That haunts my wild and restless mind

I shall forge along to build my dream
On the hills beyond the rising sun

CHIN CE

BLACK ANGEL

When the fever of the world
has hung upon
the beatings of my heart
I have spent joyless days
in solitude
When nature balms the body
on the banks of
dreams
in spirit 1 have often
turned to you
. .. black angel
When the mind reefs
on the lagoon
in the margin of a bay
I have meeting with your voice
Oh you angel of sea,
day and doom
pilgrimage your life through
this green perpetual landscape
for your holy love
vexes meditation
with extreme silentness
and the moon shines
in the void of night.

CHRIS   NWAMUO

VALENTINE

Come O my weary mistress
Fear not the barks of death
Knocks of extinction on my door
Freeze my heart not
Scorn the sinister birds.

Our oblation to Cupid fouled
Season hearts bloom in Venus moisture
Partner's seratium honour hollow elegy
Others audience to re-enactment
Drama in cities of Japan
To join the elevated lovers
Alas! Unaligned souls.

Triple baptism of the earth
More, I shall crave your shuddering warmth
In clasped souls and frames
Flight into ethereal bliss
Down down
Regret smoulders

KAYODE OGUNFOLABI

SOUL-KIN

The delightful has befallen me
for your belly-deep laughter
possess these hours of vibrant poetry
hours of nurturing lilacs
excavating the essence of history
on a beach front

I am arrested by breezy bike rides
in the war-red sun
I'm awed by the truth
of plants grown up in their youth
I write, exhilarated by the sloshing freedom
resounding dams of the rainbow spirit
Beneath brilliant nights

tenderness becomes the jack plane of
rough diamonds
the rhythm of an eternal gospel
in your stride, tangerine man
in the star light.

TOYIN ADEWALE

SOULMATES

Time drops off
Distance too
You step into my dream
We listen silently to the rice fields

Somewhere
A song comes
Of yester affairs and yesterdays
I should answer
But I don't
I laugh
And step into your arms

Infancy is gone
Truancy too.
Then
Besides
We don't need
Love affairs anymore

Now
We have grown up to this:
Soulmates.

JOYCELENE   OKORO

REQUIEM
(For SAP & Co)

TOMORROW:
We shall all remember
Many a thing with wetly laughter
We shall recall
The snake's poisonous
Bite at the monetary forest.

TOMORROW:
Time shall tell tales of
Foreign cowries
Tossing up blinding dust
Into our eyes
I know
We shall recollect
When questions were without answers
Why is it that we all are dying
Before the promised recovery of market laughter
Time shall tell of promises
Unfulfilled at the river bank
Losing our lives to live again
Yet many have gone the ancestor's way
And none, none has ever returned.

OBYNNA CHYLEKEZI

CANDLELIGHT   III

How bright you are
Little flame that flickers in this cave.
How lively your countenance
Glowing with excitement
When the sweet breeze
Sweeps over you.
How comfortable your warmth
That sweetly caresses me
Clothing me against the cold

What life giving light radiates from you!
What beautiful patterns
We make on the walls
What calamity, what hazards?
What disaster, what doom
Would befall mankind
If you were not there

And how can I ever face
The world without you?

BASSEY   U. BASSEY

OUT OF LOVE

Many things he hates to do
Under the sun's monocle
For self-esteem or decency
Many things he hates to do
Under the earth's spectacles
For ego and for pride.

But behind closed doors
He makes a spectacle
Of a dog or a horse
Many things he does
In reckless abandon
Ambling to Everest
And swimming the Nile
Prowling a liar
And milking a tigress
Just out of love
But out of reason
Many things he may do for love
But the chameleon treads the earth
Cautions only out of love
Thread the heart with sense
For reason may sew the world
A safe garment for love.

TAMMY EGWE

COLOUR HIM LOVE

It matters not one bit to me
What colour He is
He made all things
In all the blends
A sea of colour bursts
Adorns His universe
It matters not to me at all
What colour His eyes or hair

He takes the colour of comfort
When I am down
He is colour of strength
When I am weak
My Lord is coloured courage
When I'm afraid
His arms are coloured warmth
When I'm alone

His colour is Love
From morn till night
His wisdom is Love
And love his eyes
His lips speak love
And love his care
A rainbow of His love
Encircles me today

EBELE OFOMA EKO

OKONKO
(Ancestral Call)

The ominous night heralds Okonko
Reverberations of discordant gutturals
Of ancestors honoured to sup
Relating in spirit tongues only the initiate knows
Night's harvest bag is fall of do's and don'ts
And what mortal dare refuse this ancestral call?

We have returned to our duty
We have trudged through the thick-thin of dense
Nneochie
We neither trembled at the forest- quaking wilds
Nor the poisonous hissing of the slithering velds

    Sweat drenched
    Strength sapped.

We return;
Each ninth moon re-enacted
We pour generous libations
Of throat- burning liquid fires
To split ear-lobes of kolanuts and alligator peppers
To our fathers;
From whose loins we sprung and forces
Arise all, Ukwunta, Okwuzuruike, Nkpaka,
Okom digi di gi di and others
Don your beautiful embroidered masks
Come, sup from your beloved's fingers.

Ye ancestor listen and note
To us belong showers of blessings
Bread fruits of obedience
Wash and watch our aching soles in its jaunty
wandering
Bless also the fool and ignorant
To learn the true wisdom of the sages

CHIDI-EBERE   OGBO

NNEOCHIE

My pen's tears overflow in respect
Mother of the expansive marshland
Woman of the wide forested zones
        Greetings!
Oh Nneochie; ancient of mothers
Grand superitendent
Of communal ethos
Half clothed and flabby flapping breast
        Custodian of Ohia Nneochie

        Protectress,
            Hear her at twilight roar in anger
Responding to greeting from scions of the soil in season
Softly, gently not scare
As the young and carefree thread unaware
But the venerable old pause to acknowledge
You who tradition held single handedly checked
Menace of mercenary incursion during the war

CHIDI-EBERE   OGBO

MOTHER

Your hand, full moon
of the still nights,
soothes my feeble cheeks

When the tenderness of your heart
courses
soft and sweetly down my youth
to heal its wanton weal.

You immerse me
in the river of the valley
filled with ripples
of ever flowing love.

You let my hands
clasp around your arm
my ears between your breasts.

And ever after
far away from home, mother,
shall I flow this way
in the golden water of your life.

CHIN CE

CANDLELIGHT III

How bright you are
Little flame that flickers in this dark cave.
How lively your countenance
Glowing with excitement
When the sweet breeze
Sweeps over you
How comfortable your warmth
That sweetly caresses me
Clothing me against the cold.

What life giving light radiates from you!
What beautiful patterns
We make on the walls
What calamity, what hazards
What disaster, what doom
Would befall mankind
If you were absent
And how can I ever face
The world without you?

BASSEY   U. BASSEY

INSPIRATION

Comes like molten gold
snake-soft transparency
as flimsy polythene tit
filled with the milky fluid

Writhes along the garden
park of pink and pollen grains
to kiss my feet
in a soft and powdery touch

I step unto the golden
rubbery back borne
in its ripples to unfurl
as the red rose buds
and the green grasses

The spilling streams and
murmuring brooks mingle
in the music of the flowing
wind, and I become-

One with the glitter of the water
to uncoil long and timeless
In the deep beyond

CHIN CE

GIVE ME BACK

Sapped, sapped, sapped my soul
wild winds with withering waves
have eaten up my flesh

bony, skeletally bony, left I with
ulceration – from hunger
yet, my hope rose
with libations poured
give me back O day

of my sages gone who prided in
their sweet after the sweaty
harvest of the seeds of soil.

OBYNNA CHYLEKEZI

CHARCOAL

Burn,
      Charcoal burn
      Your indelible flame
      The canopy flame.

In this era of pious tyranny
Of humanity fighting to
Exterminate one another
An era unabridged inequality.

Burn,
      Charcoal burn
      Your indelible flame
      The canopy flame.

Survival is priced
Sellers tyrants
Beggars the wretched of
The earth

Burn,
Charcoal burn
Your indelible flame
The flame of truth.

TION BARUK ENDE

CONFUSION

cobwebs of memories
cling limpidly
with dissonant vocables
while destiny creates
a pattern of haste.
new days are filled
with intricate uncertainties;
waiting, scrutinizing
yet, determined
to fill the void
with prodigal eccentricity
once certain
that the untended fences
will be there in coloured dreams
but skeptical that
what once was
shall never be more ...
instinctive hands
of emotional parasites
hold fearful equipoise
in whips of strict rituals
echoing
the characteriological weakness
of apothesized demagogues.

CHRIS   NWAMUO

BOUND IN CHAINS

They stop as they run
heavy footed legs of nature
to look at the caring eyes
of a rich empty world.
... the wheel of death rolls by,
refusing to crush them,
the rubbish of the earth
they run as they stop
hungry and tired
the burden of the world
on their sweet weary backs
... another wheel horns away
veiling them with
the brown dust of life
still they run as they sweat
cleaning the dust
breathing hard
with a futile hope
to embrace a tomorrow
bound in chains.

CHRIS   NWAMUO

CONTEMPLATION
by the graveyard

Troubled heart on a cool even
Forced me out of bed well woven
To somewhere below the living
To the quiet city of joy and sadness
Crowed mind groping in the dark
Of life, lit up with understanding
As the moon lit with the night.

The quiet city below the living
Inhabited by slumber still
Fast array of white mansions
White without but dark within
Silent conversation not to be heard
Transmitted beneath the earth

So dust is dust at last
The meretricious chameleon
Failed to display its garments,
Monetary is below the soil
And it looked so far from him.

Igbokoyi my neighbour
Hide is not your breath,
Here is dark already
I knew death would come
Not the way it came.
O that I knew the way
Of death; and blocked
It with my values'
Mind not, monetary
Dust is now dust
Valued only for the block
Let dead remain dead
And the broken cord of brotherhood
Be knotted.
Great is the birth of the great
Great their exploits
Great their acquaintances
Great their living
Oh great is the death of the great!
And this shepherd- deep awareness
Goad me along
I chewed the curds of reading
Once death
Once judgement
After death's repentance
God's throne visitation

Death, ageless bridge
To Jerusalem and hades
O' passion, are you yet leading me?
When powerful men die of want of power
Wise men of want of wisdom
And in this golden tomb in the
Wake of me; with the inscription
Of gold
"Here lives the ashes of Zimri
Who fought like fire?
Yet consumed by fire';
Lies some distance below."
I saw the white herons
Perch on a glowing grave
Which carries the inscription
"The bones of the great rot not
On this we shed our wrath
For Ahith-Ophel the counsellor
Who dies of want of counsel!"
And I in complete transfiguration
Became one of these sleeping ghosts
My dust mingled with their spirits
Their spirits lectured my curious dust
Who relentlessly asked:
"Why must I lie below the living?"

Living dust, you lie below
As a mark of honour
For the wreckage lies low
And no one cares
As for the inhabitants;
So when the mortal
Is dilapidated with age
Or crushed somewhere
In the mill of struggle
The mortal enters the world
Unknown lives for ever
In heaven or hades.

Then you mortal
That dwells within my mortal
Control well this
That after your abdication
He dwells not long
In this quiet grave
Ten and eight years ago
You dug your way in
Weary of this misty weather
You will dig your way out
Then bound hand and legs
As the yam stem binds its prop
This your nest is beside the dug out
There the mortal digs his way out
And dust heaps over dust
Now the day is old beyond trust
Hasten me home before dusk.

OLUMIDE   AKINNIMI

ANCESTORS

Why my ancestors
Why are you quiet now
When things are going wrong?

You called the rains and they obeyed
In the heart of darkness
You roused your dying children

Why my ancestors?
Why are you silent now
When things are going wrong?

Our lives are no longer safe
Your children are in a prison
And things are no longer the same

Why my ancestors?
Why are you silent now
When things are going wrong?

TION BARUK ENDE

SING NIGHTINGALE

Sing, sweet song
Let it sound fine
Nightingale, sing
Sing for peace
And for love
Great tunes
Make the mind,
Sweet memories.

Night and day
Let the song go on
You are heard
Pipers of sweet waves:
In the corner
Someone's in love
Listening to you
Sing of nature

The preacher
Carries his books
Talks inconsistencies
And veers off the truth,
But today you sing
As tomorrow and forever
The same tune as ever

M.M CHUKWU

CARVED IN HIS PALM
(for Hokehe)

See!
Your tears are in my bottled stored
And when you grieve and feel distraught
My love fails not to flow

See!
I've carved you in my palm
And as my arms are round your wound
So is my love for you

See!
On my bossom do I carry you
And under the wings of eternal light
I shield my child from fright

See!
I've called you by my name
Before I clothed the heights in light
Or flung the stars in space

See!
I set my love on you my child
From hills of dung and miry clay
I took and washed you clean

See!
I make all things new
Even you
My precious one.

EBELE OFOMA EKO

SOLITAIRE

On valentine day
in the scramble for life
I drop joy scarves
on a bus gone crazy
        Let it be me
                alone

I clamp my eyelids
in the whirl of a hunt
a troubadour in dust haze
I'm cocooned in a haze
        Let it be me
                alone

When weary from hunting
I drop on the earth
harsh paper wipes the beads
of my aspirations
        Let it be me
                alone

at the junction of fare-wells
unanswered letters, hugs cut
with the precision of thunder
        and if it be me
                alone...

TOYIN ADEWALE

HE CALLS ME LOVE
(for Ugo)

He calls me love
Gives beauty for ashes
Gladness for tears
Praises for weariness
And this clay called me
between His shoulders bears

He calls me love
says rise and shine
he whispers in gold
"I'll polish you
You are a jewel, My love
You'll shine in my crown"

He calls me love
And daughter of a King
He clothes me in light
gives wings to my words
"The Pearly Gates," He says to me
"Shall swing for you my love."

EBELE OFOMA EKO

LAGOS

Wake me up in the dead of night.
I want to hear the music
of my neighbours at party
the noise of buyers and sellers
at Ipobo night market;
and the shouts of footballers
sweating it out under street lights
on the roads of Ajegunle.

Wake me up in the dead of night.
I want to hear the sound of screeching tyres;
the eerie gunshots of night marauders;
the alarm signals of night watchmen;
and the jagged rhythm of police patrol vans.

Lagos never sleeps
And tonight I'll keep her company.

ISAAC UMUNNA

UMUAHIA

The call went forth
And I heard it
It is a far call, distant
But a clear call, distinct

It is a war cry
The dead and living call
Their voices blend
Enticing invitation to war

The giant is asleep
The snoring is heard abroad
The groaning clear and loud
Anxieties fill the air
The neighbourhood is confused
Activities come to a head
But the giant will soon awake

The neighbourhood shall be agog
The people shall take up arms
The people shall win the victory
God will fight on our side

OSITA EBIEM

ABUJA

From Abu, the Emir
Created
A city side of Niger.

Travelling north
I saw the Capitol

To the sky stood the head rock of ages
Abuja!
Native with many children

M. O'BROWNE

THE RETURN
(Poets' version)

The tyres have screeched
nonstop on the tar
the dusty blur of leaves
fleeting fronds
and racing clouds
take their flight

Fly my friends now

Calabar lies beyond
your raucous roaring
and loud giggling
are faintly echoes...

Aba is a backdrop too
in the slapping rush
of violent wind
whirling away my breath
As momentum propels
to Isiala
with the turn of gear
at Ugba junction.

Fly away lone chimney
at Ubakala, through
harmattan's misty eye.

It's mud and bare
bricks in Ossa
riding Koloko's
gully-ridden roads
and half-fallen posts
battered and very bruised...

They fly away – memories
in the mental screen
and a chapter of life
shall be finished
with the journey's end.

CHIN CE

MALABO

Malabo pulsating with life
I can never forget you
The pain and laughter still rings
Of Malabites
Moulding deprivations into laughter

I still see and hear
And feel the frowziness of the rooms
The cranky bunks
Gutters over flowing
Paints peeled like calluses

Queues to pee and
Pooh and clean up
The sagging laundry wires
On weekends
The blast of chatter-boxes
And plates of cold *eba*
The endless waits for taxi
Buses bikes or *akauke*
Getting soaked in early morning rain
Pants books and all

Race for lectures and seats
Glamorous glances
From Malabresses
Those night parties and walks
Mmm…kisses
And fingers rolling down
Those little whispers and noises
And the loosening of clothes...
All for that, my Malabo,
My heart yearns for thee.

UGOJI NWABUEZE

ONITSHA

What you see is real,
People, wares and money
All corners revealed
In this disorder
And pride
Even if prey
Among these people
Who build their powers
On pillars of pain
Agile, energetic
They beat the limits
And from their pains
Make the millions

MADUANWUSI   CHUKWU

THE CHILD

The little child
In a cold morning
Walks innocent path
To school; she wades
Through water pool
And dangers
Clad in red and blue
With a suit
Bag once, twice
Then gradually
Out of sight.

OMOLAYA OGUNGBEMI

THE WIDOW

The chime –
Of the Sabbath bell calls
Morning holds its own
Clad in sullen outfit
Black, dark to mourn
The widow struts on
With two nurslings
To the sermon
A word, two exhortations
To appease the sickened soul.

The muddy splash
(it rained sometimes)
Won't stop her mission.

A mask of innocence
Beguiles each step
Each to the house
That houses God
The kids brisk away
While the widow woman
Steers the way.

OMOLAYA OGUNGBEMI

SILENT SNAKES

In this abode of snakes, assorted
from the sluggish, and the slow, dotted
To the swift and sharp, spotted
We found ourselves planted.

A vicinity of diverse silent snakes
very very silent snakes
All over the place
Unwearily watching every step.

Bethren,
safety, here lies in a silent step.

KING AGWU UDE

KABUKABU

How true my ears tell
A finger wants you-
Waged out! Or
Is my hearing silly?
When our route can't
But spot you ply Ajegunle-Maroko
To ease our mobile burden
And veer Ikoyi-Obalende
To ignore social ladder.

      It will be phony
If you are phased out
      Not funny
      If not left to live.

You at the helm
I plead save us
Your cacophony "Give
To the peasants theirs
As to them" because
The man on the street
Is without complaint
Married to kabukabu.

OMOLAYA OGUNGBEMI

LAGOS RAIN

Little, Little, Little
Drops of rain
Generously make
A mighty
Terribly tearfully tumultuous
Traffic lagoon
In Lagos.

OBYNNA CHYLEKEZI

SHOOT ME FAST

Objection my lord
My tongue stands trial.
My song, not my sense.

The end is here but
I rejoice in the past
Spent like Awoko
My sweet lashing tongue
Spares not your rot.

It shall come to past but,
Who dares cast the leading stone
In this sport of fate?

The end is near
My back to the stake
My head shoot to shred
Let the gun speak
And spell my end
Gun man, faster.

OKEY   IFEACHOR

THE HARVEST

Which barn
The grains of requiem
Carnival quietus
Searing cacophony of morbid cortege.

Silent ages
Down earth entrails
Secret tears of earth
By tempestuous seething of boiling blood.

Cat's fangs dearth's scythes
On winsome vultures bore
Munching maundering lips
And faded subtlety.

Exalted fleas in ivory tower flocked
Thuds of smiles
On blazing terrace of mercury
Prods consistent embers.

GBEMISOLA   REMI ADEOTI

SKY REFUSES PLEA

Heavy under visor of mist
Sole eye of the sky in vain rebellion
To reveal its torrid cauldron
But the sky sweeps mirthlessly
Hauled into soused nests
And darts in the throat of gasping earth.

The earth masks merry cheeks
Drought reviles its arms
Osseous shoots slump in euphoria
Gluttonous land gulps
Deep into scalded offshore
Glut, all prowl pleading
Not consoled. Now!

An imminent dawn
Fiercer drought'll overthrow the showers
And drought with all its armaments
Sack smiles, fix frowns
Tender plums wilt
Giant shrubs wither
In its arms
And all life shall lie in state.

KAYODE OGUNFOLABI

RAIN

The trees dance in tune
As the wind haul and pull
Bringing the rain
That shatter and patter
As they pelt on roof-tops

Sweeping swooping dirts and all
Its mobile devices
Jostling in a joyous swoop
Thundering lightning
As the rain comes falling down.

The mobile stationary and
Tarmac gleam
For never a day as bright
As today
Little lane its road
Deeper deeper
As the rain comes bubbling by.

A splash and slash
As they cascade
In the rush; as they bubble
And rumble, and slur and babble
Along the gully
Heralding the slugs
They took off the soil.

KAYODE OGUNFOLABI

RAINBOW

Seven wonders curve
On the eastern horizon
Telling the tale of secrets
The beauty of colour
Put a meaning to matter.

The great sign of the sky
Heralds the seasons of
Bounteous expectations
Even in the sign and know

The good and bad in light
Decomposure
Three for and three against
But one is the middle bearer.

MICHAEL   O'BROWNE

A STAR

When the vestiges of darkness
Peep into the bowls of the earth
Denatured cows and dual eyes
See not; only
Putting a veil, ah this veil.

The blind stumbles and cries
In a pang of pain
Remorse tells in him
His thoughts become gloomy
And doom lurks in the dark.

But up the sky above –
Twinkling luminous smiles
Of the galaxies
Doom and nature live
They transcend the veils of ignorance.

M. M CHUKWU

MOONLIGHT NIGHT

Out in the field
Gazing up above
At night to the moon
A luminous disc
Shining tenderness.

When one in tune
With nature's beauty
Sees the sanctity
Of your serene glow
Peaceful he should be.

In the moonlight night
The wise sees
The innocence
Of forms and tranquility
Persuades the earth...

In meditation
The wise sits
On his feet
He oversees
The beauty of creation.

Graceful moon
Sends its radiance
To beautify creation
So love will dwell.

M. M CHUKWU

RIPPLES

Ripples dancing
In ever-widening
Circlic sliding
Like leaves
In autumn gales
Of shattering beau.

Gently and whoosh
A drop and *awhaash*
A throw and some wheeze
Rippling fine and smooth.

Nature's so good
Nature's so kind
A too-gate
Of existence
Lies a guardian law...

In this great ripple
An infallible law
Of nature rings true –
From a seed
Many a more is gotten.

Just like a pebble throw
Of many countless
Wide ripples
In nature's deep ocean.

M .M CHUKWU

AFTER A STORM

Quaking squirrels
    In drench
From nature's
    Torrential fall
As they clenched
    For safety
Is it curse from deity?

    Torpidly
Strayed rats wobbled to hole
    From day to dawn
Tortuous walks.

There's two to life;
Be drowned in storm,
    Or hold to straw
Till calm...

The eyes watery drop
Is no to sores.
        Rainy days not a life.

When climbed the steep.
        The shine is due
For after storms
        Comes a calm.

MICHAEL   O'BROWNE

CHILDREN OF AFRICA

Here they are
Sucking on the way
The back of their mother
In the hot sun like heat of fire.

In tattered cloths
Bare legs
And bereaved uncombed hair
They play around
Their heads as big as the elephant's
Their neck as long and tiny as the ostrich's
Their ribs showing like unfed cows
With a stomach like a pregnant woman's
Whose hands as tiny as her legs.

After crossing the red sea
They finally come to stay
And to survive in the rain
They move about to sell...

In the sun
With buckets on their heads
Searching for water
In the dark
With candle they read
To sleep
They solace under the bridge.

Oh! See them holding tightly
To their stomach
They are weeping
Begging for money
"Please ten kobo for food."

Oh African child
Weep no more
Learn the hard way and be wise
For hard times do not last
But tough people do.

MICHAEL   O' BROWNE

ON HER NATURAL STATE

Commissioned photograph means more
Than snapping what the camera sees
So they arrested him:
He snapped her naked
Photographed on a door
Entering the hospital lab.
Armed with a begging bowl,
A puddle in the background,
Her eyes flooded with tears
Her head double the size
Of her whole body,
Her tummy swollen
Her thin legs creaking,
And in the background still,
Her mother and father,
Her brothers sisters and cousins,
All her stature,
Number only twenty eight
Without counting the one
Strapped sleeping on the back
Of the pregnant mother
For whom the doctor
Has diagnosed twins.
Below it the artist had inscribed:
TOWARDS 1992.

ADEGOKE

131

THE VILLAGE MUEZZIN

The heat hung, rasping
The air still, unstirring
The goat and cattle are away, grazing
Only the children, occasionally crying
And the fowls forever scratching.

And there he stands
– amid the stone formation –
his mouth agape, his brown teeth
in his divine duty.
His freshly washed feet too clean
Beneath his ochre rigs and hulls

His cry, shrill and piercing,
Scratches the fouls, gathers the faithful.

BASSEY   UDE BASSEY

ECOMOG

What is this I heard again
Of ECOWAS gone to Liberia
Struggling to capture Monrovia.

Then I asked,
"What have they gone to do?"
A voice answered:
"Three children of one mother
and father are fighting.
Two oppositions of khaki and mufti
Face each other."

Then I asked
"Who will stop the shedding of the blood?"
I heard the voice say
"ECOMOG"
But the twins have seized their tools
To face the intruder
What song of woe is this?
That my soldiers are being killed
My people kidnapped and dehumanised?

I saw the Angel of destruction over the land
Vultures spreading over the land
Their cattle died!
Their people died
  Paragons of beauty in the land
  Destroyed
  And the land is desolate

  And I asked,
  "Who will rule a wasted land?"

ADEGOKE

AFRICA

Africa, my Africa,
Africa my motherland,
Africa the land of the black race,
Torn in a conflict
Africa of high and low lands,
Africa of thick forest and shrubs,
Africa in which abound many rivers,
And natural wealth
Bountiful and splendid
Africa, my Africa,
A race struggling within
For a place in the sky;
Wither do you go now?

When the white race
Had lunged upon you
A cloud overshadowed you,
In a wave of cultures
Like the mighty roars of the Atlantic
Across the beaches of Lagos.
You were torn apart,
Body and soul,
In bits of disgusting rags...

When believers and ministers of imported religions
Go back to their African roots
You are an edifice of tattered cloths
When teachers and students of white knowledge
Go up and down in the mystery of the same
You are an effigy of the past.
When the series of the western trials
Have failed us as we have failed them.
You are in chaos.
When orthodox medicine swallowed tradomedics
Struggling to re-emerge.
You strangulate between them.

When laws are turned upside down
And jungle justice and witchcraft reign.
You too are turned to rags
Metaphysical science still
Has a place in our wars.

When tradition goes on
In the presence of foreign marriage.
You are in a great confusion.

Africa, my Africa,
Africa, my fatherland,
Africa of past proud warriors,
Africa then and now,
Africa of the black race,
Torn in conflict
Knowing not how to mend the rags.

And now, arise, Africa!
Wake up from your slumber, Africa!
You either be up or down the ladder
The present midway takes your breath.

OSAYANDE   IGBINEDION

MY CULTURE

Last night
I dreamt a bad dream
I dreamt my ancestors weeping
At this years gathering
Weeping for my having lost
What they left me to keep.

OBYNNA CHYLEKEZI

VANITY

Six heavy strides
Toward the charging bull
At the equator
Arms akimbo
      I ask
The howling wind
The charging bull
      Who am I?
The wind whistles back
To my burning ears
      You are a man
Muscle-armed, hairy-chested
I say to the whirlwind
      I am the rock
Whose spark first gave men
The warmth of fire
      I am the fox
Whose cunning feet beat
The skilful hunter traps
      I am the green mountain
Whose navel caresses only
The hands of strong climbers
      I am the high sea
In whose strong bossom lies
The strength of a thousand lions
      I AM A MAN!

II

Time calls
Scanty harvest stares back
At my staring eyes
Time calls

Time calls
As thin snake bones decorate
My ancient hunting gun

Time calls still
As I gaze at the drifting wind
And the falling sun.
Time calls aloud
And with glazed eyes
I ask the amber rays
What am I?
This time;
Silence greets
My prostrate self
And the withered roses whisper
Into my closed ears
YOU ARE A DEAD MAN!

CHEKWUBE   CHUKWU

DIPLOMATIC SMILE

A dazzling smile,
Lightning-like;
And like lightning
Fascinating but facetious.

KING AGWU UDE

NOBEL PRIZE

Alfred Nobel
Plucked the fruits of destruction
From the trees of knowledge
And sold to us
Bags of dynamite.

Now
We the disciples of chaos
Let loose the doors of war
And win prizes of defeat
In every victory!

CHEKWUBE CHUKWU

EVOLUTION

When I was a child
I saw the world
In rose colours
And imagined
These mysteries, these myths
That surround every space
As time tells its tale
       Now time flies and spent
       Mysteries fade
       The light within shines
       Ah, its nature its life
       But fools are deceived
I am flying with time
So this true nature glows
Then I rise beyond the space
And be this shining being
Ripe with age
There are no mysteries
And wisdom reveals it all.

CHEKWUBE   CHUKWU

THREADS

Threads of unholy fertility
Litter like Iroko trees
Planted by scavengers
Of immature fruits.
Keeps busy their sutured cases.

The wrinkled
Beasts of earthly epithelium
Drain their piles,
Scavenging courageously.
Polluting bowls, spilling their contents
Whose weak feet step from womb to earth

Had the shadows
Cast by divine day sky
Showered their rays clearly
The echoes of these weak drums
Would have seen their way home.
And the arena free of drummers
Who throw a yolk into every beat.

M.M CHUKWU

2000 AD

The boundless morrow
With a thick fog of hope
Two thousand we hail thee!

A season that never ends
When the whistling sirocco
Shall blow dew-drops
Of Iroko
And the cloak of plenitude
Shall veil the life-long lack.

Abode for rag-pickers
Gratis
Knowledge for nescient
And many lost in the mire
Fulfilled shall their desire

But
Will you be reached
By languid trekkers
All weary and chilly brained?

CHINEDU NWOSU

WHO CARES?

O who would care for me in a distress?
Who would care to save the helpless?
When men came into the world
They invented and shaped the world
That the poor may live in misery
Even their offspring live in luxury
Who would care for the meek
In pains they suffer to seek
All that does come from heaven
Let peace to them be given
For all they live to see
Are the things God has made free
Like light, air, and water
Let them not forever totter.

ANTHONY UBI

WHAT'S IN THE WORD

What's in the word?
Artists have it more
      Mayakovsky
          Sergei Esenin
Cheeny Coker
…   Okigbo
      what became of them?

Could words be swords
Festering in a mindwound
Or the brain a balloon
Blown much to dissension
That thought finds strange byways
Leaving the soul empty?

Poets unallowed to print,
or misinterpreted
What became of them?

      Allowed to thin
      But not to print
      Brains run risk
      Insanity a bedfellow
      For these words...

147

What's in this word?

Playwrights wanting words
To prop inspiration
Run around naked in closets
Soaking selves in alcohol

Unable to refrain from saying
What he thinks
And saying what he thinks
For them to relay
What they think he thinks
Artists make our words
Go mad, go sad.

What is in these words?

Men making money
Rarely go mad
Poets smithing words
Rarely are glad:
>Divorcing wives on phone
>Committing suicide on ropes
>Shooting selves in hotels
>Making pacts with alcohol
Obsessed with the spirit
Artistes don't make money.

Brother, tell me,
What's in this word?

MUSA ALANI

LIFE

A flux:
Sweet smiles
After bitter tears
Sweet smiles
Before bitter tears
Flurries of excitement
Flurries of alarm.

OBYNNA CHYLEKEZI

A FERTILE SOIL TO TILL

The green-fingered farmer
In his endless search for a maiden piece
Wanders hither and thither
Before the advent of the rains.

His old parcel of land
Acquired chaste with zest,
Ploughed and watered
For years with zeal

Now lies stale and waste
Slipper-breasted and dejected,
Incredulous of her abandonment,
She mopes and moans

As her ageing ploughman,
Digger and horsepipe in hand
Goes from interior to interior
Exploring a fertile soil to till.

KING AGWU UDE

THE SEARCH

The work piece left the matrix
Then the search began
Intense and perturbing
Crushingly painful
As the pang at birth.

It is a mixture
of love and hateful pain
of life and death.

The real and the chimera
Hope and hopelessness.

Search the ultimate depth
The storehouse of knowing
The keys of the kingdom
The flint of a bold face.

OSITA EBIEM

REST NOT IN PEACE

No don't wish me rest
Do you think I lax all day?

Never pray me that
In anger I shall burst
Forth from the grave
I want to move ahead
Above this plane and all.

Why should I rest
When I feel motion all
Around me
Do you think I sleep and freeze
As soon as my lids close?

Wish me no rest
For my journey's sake
Pray me to stand the pilgrim's
Test and have a taste
Of all my ugly seeds
sown there, where you are.

Rest me not in peace
But let me nestle
    To break the many tentacles
That hold me down.

No don't pity me!
You multiply my guilt
Or give me accolade
I hardly deserve.

Your good will do
Not the open air prayer
But the luminous rays
Of your godly thoughts.

OLUMIDE   AKINNIMI

MORE KINGLY

What can we call thee, with
All the sensation, the
Hustle and the bustle, when
Not knowing was no knowledge.

Like ants bearing their king
How in his sealed dark blue truck
They lay siege, on the
Central Bank past pedestrians
And commuters; the whole city
Must rock to the tune
Of police sirens, blaring
Shock into all who watch, knowing
One lifeless thing had just passed
And how more kingly than a king!

M O'BROWNE

HOMEWARD BOUND

How best could it be
Homebound we are
In death lives our home
On a stormy sea trip
Like the millipede, our grave
Though death, we are
Homebound
Every place, day and time!

OBYNNA CHYLEKEZI

HEARTS

My heart fluttered
Like a strangling bird
Desperate to keep a beat
With the fading tempo.

Thoughts of futures
Unknown
Stretch the shred of my fears.

I start out solemnly
From my small room
To the sea-side…

And I saw
Where the fishes swam
And played hide and seek
The night birds flew
They went in search of food.

I saw
Where little rats
scurried in search of meal
And sped past in lovers race…

And I knew then
That tons of my plight
Are like a drop of water
In the midst of the ocean
Suddenly, the burden is lifted
And I burst into loud fits
Of hilarious, glorious laughter.

GMT EMEZUE

FORTIETH AVENUE

Down the crowded streets below
  Lie tainted garments
  By a slush of dirt.

And winged fights impaired
  By missiles launched
  From unseen corners.

It was hard to turn
  From the cackling mob
  At Fortieth Avenue
  From four decades of vice.

And now I have come far away
  In my loneliness
Here on the towering do I strive
That nothing shall hold my hand

To surf the waves against the clouds
With the wind beneath my wings.

CHIN CE

BETRAYAL

We left the warmth
Of our heart
And the promise of our ancestors.

In the chill of howling wind
With thirst and quest
We carried our hearts
To bear our dreams

And assuage our sorrows
To the civilised hut

We bruised our knees
Reciting litanies
Surrendering with cheers
The contents of our hope.

But when I looked
I saw him
In his papal garb
And shrieking flickers of greed
In his eyes.

CHIKA AYOGU

TREASURE ISLAND

Behold the majesty of
My treasure island
Her glow is the hot
Cinder of chocolate moon
And her brain
A prickle wave of
Poignant sensations
She is the furrowed cloud
Of flowered dreams
And her beauty
A powdery flame
Undimmed in the sea.

CHIKA AYOGU

JOS

I like to be like
these rocks of the endless age
crouched and slumbering
in the Northern heat.

How long is your meditation
you giants bored and
(all around the greenery)
barely seeing.

Through seasons of wind and mist
nothing can rile your colloquium
grim monarchs
with the clouds of guards above.

CHIN CE

WHIRLWIND

Caught in the centre
The whirlwind blows
With facts and fiction
Piercing into me
Round, round, and round
My brain runs
As the whirlwind soars.

CHIKA AYOGU

MY BABY

I can see the being in you,
child of mine, that speaks
this gurgling rush of love.

I can see it in your smile:
this steady gaze of dearest you
like an open page.

Your brown, chubby cheek;
soft and wet: these lips
Your wide and toothless laugh
and fist-clenchingrip all tell —

Of the Word
embodied
in this chapter of your life.

Let the light of your crown
shimmer with wisdom
as of the Masters ascending
in the radiancof the ether.

Not emptied
in the vagrancy
of the rabble
and their bearded rouser.

Yes shun the vanity
of Hypocrites and
clay footed gods.

For here between light and dark
lies the bridge, beyond:
the dazzle flight of angels.

Here in your eyes my dear
like a marble
in sparkling water

In this dot of shimmering light
innocence lies like a flower bud.

And what are you, soul,
but the joy and freedom of your being?

CHIN CE

THE SLUM DWELLERS

We are the dregs
Of a society since decayed
Trapped in a miasma
Of airless heat

We are the edge
Of a society
Long gone away
Endowed with swarms
Of mosquitoes and bugs
Who dive on us
Like century old jets
To assault our sleep
And prey upon our skins

We are the floors of life
Heaped in teaming multiples
Into shacks of civilisation
Bestowed with the perfumes
Of slimy stagnant slums
Of blocked drains
Suffused with
Putrid
Human waste...

Yes we are also part
Of a suffocating system
Who must be seen
To instill greatness.

We are the scavengers
Who must watch
Refuse dumps
And to sweat
Round the year
To maintain the smooth
Dreams of greedy vermin.

We are yet
Men of iron muscles
Who must toil like ants
To oil the great ship
Only to watch our
Progenies die
On floor mats
And our stomach
Stout in hunger's
Sweet agony.

So we are
Slum dwellers
Blessed with hordes
Of bloated children
Long wasted in infancy
By the unchanging course.

CHIKA AYOGU

SONG OF BLEEDING HEARTS

I see

        your harvest of blood and hate
        and skulls and broken bones
        and bleeding hearts and throats cut.

I see

        the skull and ghastly grin
        fixed behind your plastic smiles.

I smell

        the stench of swollen corpses
        and fetid breath of death
        behind your rousing colognes.

I feel

        the heart-wrenching tug
        of your red succuba lips
        and your merciless drag
        of your fallen victims
        along your razor lips.

It hurts the eyes

        the flash of your guillotine legs
        across the crests of crowned heads.

I hear
      the sighs of final breaths
      and the pop of eyes bursting
      from surprised sockets.

I hear
      the staccato
      roll of one more head
      onto a heap of rotting skulls
      you have gathered between your legs.

I clearly hear
      the silent scarlet scream
      spraying the heavens in protest,
But there you sit unmoved
Unconcerned
      cleaning and preening
      whetting your razors
      waiting like the mantis
      praying for throats
      to prey upon and bless
      with the remorseless kiss
      of your mantis razor lips.

PETER ONWUDINJO

MALABO VOICE

Who said we are blind
When the usual martial songs
Graced our wake with its bastard
Rhythm. Beret over beret.

Who said we don't know
When "liberty" is bastardised
And "freedom" to say how you know
Is stabbed with a rare blood spill.

Now the rhythm and beret are subtle
Proscriptions. Yes!
The people now in bundle
Are burnt offerings to God.

CHIKA AYOGU

TRUTH

I'm the tiding
Brutally suppressed
And covered with might
But like the smoke I
Filter and hang stubbornly
To torment and choke the devils.

I'm the conscience
Of the hapless wretch
Whose breath soothes
The frayed nerves
Of the harmless just.

I'm also the news
Whose life is a threat
To many but
Like bile
I'm bitter in taste
And adorable in action.

So I am
The armless truth
That is daily hounded
With tanks and mortars
And murdered in cold blood
Mutilated
To appease the greedy god
Of the bloated
Yet I am the sign
That must grow
To rebuild the earth
And water the field
Of abandoned values.

CHIKA AYOGU

A DIRGE OF HONOUR

Abused
He left the scattered
Huts of normal life.

Bruised
He fled from the
Barbaric spears of
Furious climbers

To the romp of
Flush carpets
And bulging pockets
But was murdered
In a secluded chamber
By remorseless greed.

Now few gather
To murmur frightfully
A dirge of honour
For the once cherished
And departed justice.

CHIKA AYOGU

THE PAUPER

I'm a pauper
Impoverished all day
      – and derided
Infested with sores and sears
Like the scarecrow in the farm
I like the stringing rags
On my back
Stubbornly cling to life
Sloppily dragging
The feet of time.
The bridge
Has become my abode
And the sea wind
A wall of defence.
By the side of the Marina
I sometimes sit
To dream over the spectacular mirage
Of limos and towers
And a sea of humanity
And lament over the day
Of my first shrill cry.
In the face of harsh odds
I still hope and pray
That even the little I eat
The priests will take.

CHIKA AYOGU

THE EARTH BREATHES

Ancients of our land
My knees touch
Your great abode.
When the milk of mother runs dry
Where again shall the child suckle?
The bird may fly
Over the wide sky but
Mother's nest is shelter still.

Great fathers –
You who imbibe in drops
I pour this wine of lamentation
Brewed in the sickness of our land ...

II

Our bellies itch, yes they twitch
Pricked by worms fed us
By our rulers – their rulers.
We drink empty words
Filtered by sweet talkers
their soothing breeze biting hard.
We are treated as children :
'Close your eyes while I deceive you.'
And helpless as a trapped rat
Our mouths are filled with our blood.

Our tongues seal with despair,
Ancient ones, we gaze upon
Our heritage
Gulped down the long throats of
Some few fattened by
Our wealth now theirs.
Coming and going in varying fashions
One purpose attaining one goal
They wear loose-woven cotton
Covering their naked lies
Telling us brazenly why they came:
'That you may die that I may live!'
They thrive on our helpless fears
Kindling our wild imagination
Our can't-help pastimes
In present moments of delusions...

III

Great sages of a blooming past,
Do not frown at us when we say –

That we, like foolish ants
Who lost their voice for the sweetness
Of honey, forgot ourselves and
Danced lame to the Judas tunes
Of our foes.

We have been castrated
   – and stupefied –
by our green-skinned brothers
Their staff is the
Metal sneeze of leaden death
And their boots shine with their havoc
      We cannot
Dance their swift music
      We cannot
watch them dance. We are
like birds in a cage
Who cannot but die
When the ration stops.

They kick us, they lash us
They put us in cells if
We dare as much as ask
Why...

IV

Why,
Listening spirits,
Are we given spittle to wash our hands
While in mid stream?
Why
Are we forced to beat our bellies
When there are ready drums for music?

We have loved our land
We fought to build it
And spilled our blood
But they have taken
The choicest parts
Leaving us the bones...

V

Yet the earth breathes
For it is the abode of the sleeping fathers
Though the air be congealed
By the blood of men,
Fathers hear me
The substance of the earth
Shall not die:
Can the tapper drown
In his own wine gourd?
Even so is the okra
Never taller than who planted it.
So let them eat now
For soon
The yam and the knife shall be ours...

Ancients of our land
Think on these words
My libation ends.

CHIJI   AKOMA

MY GENERATION

The scavengers
Form a hungry guard of honor
At the gates of heaven
Fighting flies for the waste.
Breaking their ranks
At the approach of an angel.

Unlucky generation
To depend on charity
From innocence,
What evil have you done
For surely does the just
God never punish
His own people.

BASSEY   U. BASSEY

AT THE THRESHOLD

Fall, fall and crash your limb
Fall, fall and crash below
Your flesh to the mud
Where you poke your accursed head
Fall I pray you fall!

Slow, the hunter-insects
Bury corpses the world despise
And shed a tear
To clothe the left-away.
When the night birds
Begin their nightly songs and feast
Run don't look back
But run!

Deep, yes, deep and deeper
You'll find yourself
Between the gravely pit
The devil is waiting
By the deep, black sea
Will you hold or fall
Yes, you are likely to fall.

Hold it just a while
Can you follow
The radiant thread
From the false
Devil's dark?
Hang on, pray in sight
It's small and safe
Take it at the threshold
Will it collapse?

Scream and be the alien
Succumb and be doomed
What shall you do?

Belt up, no option
Near the threshold
To the brink of collapse
Will you scream
Or succumb
Cry or fight it out.
When all the odds
Are by your side
Will you fall and fall *yakata*?

M. O. BROWNE

THE TASK

It's hanging up and dangling
My father's prophetic warning
In time I fault and refuse to care
Behold he says:
"Look up son, it's hanging!"

It's hanging up and swaying
As nights take the days by and by
In every wake
And fall when the ball's big
Behold it's hanging up.

For it's Hercules' task ahead
For he that will not buckle up
His skate now that it's dawn
But would waver till it's dusk
Behold it's hanging up.

The task ahead is hanging up
And swaying and dangling
Pull off your *agbada*
Before it falls heavily on you
For the task is hanging up.

M. O. BROWNE

ADMONITION TO THE GRAVEYARD

Silent world of ghosts
Isolated land of spirits
Here lies a generation
Of the wasted
In a cursed land that
Knows nothing
Nothing but sadness
Gobbler of the ripe.

Today, I may be your catch
Were you created only to
Consume?
I can guess that you're up
To be the mother of trillions
At the resurrection.

DEBO BABALOLA

BETRAYAL

Together we prepared the dish
With salivating mouths
Now, at the table they sit
Wining and dining
With *ashoke* sky-scraping-caps
While in the bin
We struggle for the crumbs
From the master's table
Bare rags on blithed bodies.

OKEY IFEACHOR

LADY

When I look
At your Made-in-Taiwan face
With African raw material
I quickly descend on my knees
And offer a tree of condolences
To the shamed goddess
Of African beauty.

CHEKWUBE   CHUKWU

MADAM

She came in outrageously
Sultry.
'You for knock, madam'
'Ragamuffin,' she muttered
'Address me not madam,
But blonde
Madam irritates me
Increases my ageing years
O god
I am ritzy.'
'Ridgy, *abi* ?
Madam I be African man-o!'
Confounded,…oh.
She is out.

TION ENDE BARUK

THIS FEELING
(On board the NNC ONURA)

It hits you
It grips you
It crushes
Like a huge monster
Slowly but surely
Crushing
And grinding the very
Essence of my life
Out the brimming body—

This feeling
Foreboding
Enveloping
Snuffing
Every life
Till you'd become like them
Just the way they want you:
Walking, grinning zombie.

GMT EMEZUE

MINI MINDED

What is the shame
If it is the fashion
That those who are civilized
Must move with the times?

We should not be ashamed
Of the wind blowing our nudity
Or were our parents not created so
Enjoying the apples in Eden?

That Genesis echoes this Revelation
As scales fall from our eyes
Our women now move with time
And men admire the tide.

Why should we be ashamed
Of sleeping together in parks and cares
For all we know, Abel and Cain
Were conceived out there in the garden.

If our skirts ease passages
Between skirt and laps
And we fork apples between wet lips
In open parks and gardens, what's the crime?

MUSA   ALANI

CULTURAL FOG

Father mailed me to school
He registered me
Like a valued parcel
At the post office.

Afterwards
I returned home
Not back to sender
But
Prodigally
Returned I
Before my Ala
Feverishly
Returned I
After a cold tidal current
Over the warm moist
In my vessel.

I returned
A reptile
Cold blooded
With a cultural fog.

OBYNNA CHYLEKEZI

LADIES

Blue flames,
Bellowed by bougainvillea
Arteries
Rose from my hearts: paraffin
Taper of dusking hours
They shone like
The egg-like moon
In the nest of
The sky
They show the
Ugly face
Pimple-clustered
Sheet of eczema coats
Lurking behind these
Shadows
Centuries of fossilled mat
Of adultery
They sow the
Aborted blood
Kicking in the flowing
Streams of gutter.
Baited in coy beams
Dimmed by love
Masked
But in a gingered mascara.

HENRY OBI

IN A TYPE OF QUARTERS

I heard of life, a dreary life;
A kind of life imported from far,
A life of loathsome solace
Life in a type quarters?

I knew of life, a gloomy life
A form of life that bores the liver,
Which fears to communicate
No jokes or talks, not anyway,
When they live in a type of quarters.

I saw of life, a life forlorn;
Life were you speak but hear the echo,
Life where you'll cry your neighbour's deaf
While alone, each one sits
Living in a type of quarters.

I sipped of life, a life of woe;
A life the liver is alarmed to live.
Aghast with madness in a whole girl
Or shouts of terror where the been-tos
Live in a type of quarters.

Life of the been-to, life from afar
Life of cold and deep distrust
Life best fitted where nature's cold...

Here is warm and nature mild
Here we sing and drink and laugh,
Here we greet both low and high
These we'll keep though been-tos sigh
When they live in a type of quarters.

O who would like to live alone?
To talk to self? a life of stone?
Why fear your fellows and bang the door?

We're ready to cheer when you are merry;
We're willing to admire if you're charming.
We won't be cold when you do smile
As you live in a type of quarters.

Do be of cheer and face the world,
Do look upright, lift up your chin.
You're far from those unfriendly foes,
Who jeered at you for colour and form.

There you met some race distressed
You felt misfit, inferior and odd
Brighten up! You are free from them
Though you live in a type of quarters!

PK DAVIDS

SOLITUDE
(In memory of Nnabuenyi Ugonna)

Gently like travelling clouds
mankind drifts into eternity,
generation after generation,
layers of graveyards across the world.

Think of all the pieces of cloud
sailing gently to eternity,
beautiful faces in a crowd,
honeyed voices in a passing encounter,
laughter and glitter
of teenage girls,
toddle of infants,
swaying dance of flowers.

See the tender feathers
of the butterfly,
heavenly colours
in the underbelly of the cobra,
orange membrane
in the robin's open mouth...

Hear the invisible breeze -
fleeting silver on green grass.
Lament the pain in the guts of the poor,
homeless, bemused, afraid of entangling
pathways and stones.

Feel life in the bones of elders,
soul in rocks in the heaving mountains.
Rejoice in the beauty of creation:
voices of humanity trapped in mud,
memories of loved ones lost in the wind.

ONUORA OSSIE ENEKWE

MALEDICTION FOR A MAXIMUM RULER

1

Write the poem, the Wind hailed me
Chew the bones and drink the blood
of emperors in your appetite of writing
Churn that bloodless art
and chant no more evil
about the beast; feel no more nightmares
when next you hear the creeping rumours
of minted monies exhumed.
Sing your harmless song, O poet
and ask no extinct questions
about Tyrannosaurus
and the lost incense of fats...

2

But I tried most in vain
to kill this knifing nightmare
I tried in vain to slash the cursing tongue
Not to remember the emperor of scars
who forgot his brains
in a luncheon of prostitutes...I tried in vain
Not to seek foolish questions like
who held the treasury-key
when cyclops burnt the State House
or who sprinkled the soil with seeds
of sorrow and irrigated the mind
with threats of self-succession.

3

Oh yes, I tried to believe
that his bones now simmer
in Dante's Sulfuric region
broiling in the tutorial vice
of Amin-Bokassa-Doe-Sese Seko School.
They say the emperor is dead
But his symbols dangle
Dangerously
his horsemen still ride
their own mother's widow's sisters
they hoist their pride
in hides of pretence...

4

In the emperor's trail
let there be a conference of curses
In the tyrant's praise
let cannons of fake biographies be burnt
And on the terrible soil
which swallowed the pig
let an epitaph of piss be written:
HERE ROTS NEBUCHADNEZZAR FOREVER
KING OF LOOTERS; HE WROTE HIS NAME
IN BLOOD, ON RIVERS OF BLAZING SHAME
HERE LIES THE CURSE FOREVER!

REMI RAJI

A COUNTRY WRITES HER OWN EPITAPH
(For Ogaga Ifowodo & Akin Adesokan)

From the beginning of night
      To the end of day
Vigils for Death become the new
      dance-craze of my people.

From the beginning of night...
      Kings build prisons like crooks
Around their conscience.
      They hatch new laws to sharpen old crimes

.. .To the end of day
      They wash their hands over me
Like a paparazzi of pontius pilates
      They wash their memories with wicked grins

From the beginning of night
      To the end of day
My children flee the streets
      Of sorrow and cremation...
My children flee to other lands
      Seeking the kindness of strangers.

From the beginning of year
      To the end of month
The hangman grieves over and over–

Work and underpay
His fridge is filled with tongues
    Of dangerous talkatives...
And my children grieve
    Afraid of the noose and the acid.

From the beginning of night
    Prodigals and prostitutes rape me
Till the end of day
    They seal my face with folds upon folds
Without the dream of light
    Without the hope of waking.

From sea, swamp to savanna
    I quake
From night, day to night
    I tremble, for them, my children
For no one, not even the dead
    Is safe
From these vigils
    Of a new destruction.

From the beginning of night
Till the end of day...

REMI RAJI

MAMMON WORSHIP

They fence them with iron and concrete -
those palaces of granite
built with blood money...
monuments of sin in stone!
Red-eyed security dogs
walk around them
to scare off nemesis.

Funerals of rich rogues
are for heavy feasting.
Beer and champagne aplenty
for oily throats and sticky fingers.
Security dogs chat with chicken bones.
Corpulent mouths and anuses
open and close the gates of hell.

ONUORA OSSIE ENEKWE

DICTATORSHIP

A gross beast
hauls itself across the sky
casting a heavy night over the land
crushing the spirits in sunflowers
polluting the air with its stench
of rotten tongues between molars.

A mist of despair
hangs over the blood-stained lake.
The mourning wind wafts the ashes of the
dead
and the bewildered cries
of their offspring sunset-bound
without homes.

ONUORA OSSIE ENEKWE

203

FACIAL MARKS (Post-Petrol Era)
(To the people of Mindo, Ecuador)

Facial marks help folks
Pick out members of the clan
Environmental scars traced
By seismic lines and illegal loggers
Transnational eco-devourers
Alienate us from our land
We are strangers to our own soil

Oil ducts
Tear ducts
Oil pipes
Blood veins
Pipes of conflict
Ducts of death
Pipes of blood

Facial marks beautify our folks
They help us attract and scare and show our strength
Environmental scars are death masks
Forced, alien, wicked, hateful
Slave marks, hellish scars...
Alienate us from our land
Now, we are strangers to our own soil

Come together valiant souls
Drive off evil serpents from our land
Sacred that is our earth
Link those hands across the seas
Let's block these ducts with our
Collective fists

These pipes of dreams
Of dollars and sorrows and tears
These ducts burrow into our hearts

These pipes dry our lands
These pipes drain our souls
These pipes steal our dreams.

NNIMO BASSEY

ANOTHER DOG DIED

Yesterday
It was a dog unknown
Knocked down in the day
By a Mazda brown and known
That died.

Nobody stopped for a minute
No, not even the driver, our neighbour
Not even pedestrians, mute
Shuffling to their locations of labour.

Not even pregnant women
Who know the pain of labour;
Experience, little known to men
Who, no doubt, plant the labour.

Like people having necks of wood,
Everybody walked-passed with stiffness
Not out of fright, not fear; their mood
Lovelessness and unneighbourliness.

But Brutus only
A rather civilized but abrasive dog
Yapped and barked solely
Around the remains of the dead dog.

But today, amazingly strange
Brutus lies dead
Killed outside his cage
By the same heartless Mazda.

And the world shouts, "horror!"
To stop the Mazda's deadly madness
They mount road blocks.

And build speed breakers
But soon
Very soon
The steam will be lost
The blocks and breakers wear off
And another dogged dog dies.

KING AGWU UDE

PALACE WEDDING

Where
Ignorance is the bride
And Greed is the groom
A tyrant is born.

JOE USHIE

FIRST OCTOBER

First October
and the sigh-reign runs
the race for the spoils
of peace looted from our toils

First October
and the freedom has slipped
into the pockets of the strong,
a child'scoin in crab's hole

First October
and the peasant's blood drips
from the flying Green-White-Green
greyingthe land at dawn

First October
and the walking skeletons
litter the Mercedesed streets
like mysteries exposed at noon

First October
and they look for how
to finish their loot,
we look for how to stay alive

First October:
Their day of boom
Our day of doom
Their day of birth
Our day of death.

JOE USHIE

ENCOUNTER

In innocence
I made a U-turn
At the wrong place
"Hay you! Hoi! You!
Stop there!
So you've
Taken the law
Into your hands!
Stop!"
In fright I breathed deep
Into my left pocket
And then breathed out
And he left
Taking
The law from my hands
Into his right pocket.

JOE USHIE

ADMONITION
(To a poet in crisis)

Sharpen the edges
of the word
Roll up the passion
into a grenade

And voice in thunder the agony
(of dying selves)

Let the pages tremble
with detonating phonics
like embattled fronts

And spy the wasted remains
for the eye beyond the eyes
showing how Death laughs

Here, pick up the stench
from the trench
let the meaning stink

And do not end your story
without a sigh.

OBODODIMMA   OHA

BIRDS OF THE AIR

Little creatures of God
Flying high and flying low
Singing praises unto God
For the Lord is good, you know
Shout loud your praises to God
It is good that man should know
That we owe our praises to God
For He is high and we are low

KING AGWU UDE

GOING TO SCHOOL

Bag on my back
And to mummy and daddy
I bow my bye;
and hurry out to school.
Reaching the road;
Like a pillar, I stand.
Eyes right and eyes left,
No cars coming; I cross.
Marching like a soldier,
Left right, left right.

KING AGWU UDE

GRAVEYARD

sun-dried and cold-dried
our consciences
waddle around
smell of things that dried
pour into our faces

hitting our legs
on grave of conscience
of those who have
disco-danced to death
and fall upon
our buried affluence
and there beckoning us
stands dead wealth.

E. E. SULE

TRUE EARTH'S PEOPLE
(For all friends of the earth)

True Earth's people
Revive your pens and papers
Camped in your tirade rucksacks
When men decline your heated pleas
For you are indeed
      A people of passion
      A platoon of protesters
Where would the waters run to
If not cities, when radioactive lumps
Satiate, indeed, choke the deep?
What would be the fate of the train
When dredging overturns
These hills, these fills
Shouldering the railway?
True Earth's people
Revive your pens and papers
Camped in your tirade rucksacks
For the earth won earnest enemies from
      North to south
      East to West.

ALBERT OTTO

DOWNING OUR TOOLS

O Emperor:

We pledge to live in peace
side by side
with your Skyscraper
if the eaves of your heart
does not, like tree branches
in rain, pelt us with acid rain

Our roots have no capacity
for yesterday's hell.
They thrive by today's nutrients.

O Emperor:

Give us our daily bread;
and cut the thorns planted on
our pathways.
Better the carcass
of our refineries in our palms
than under the armpits of vampires.

NGOZI OBASI AWA

RAIN

Rain in drought:

Parched earth leap to lap you up
like a hungry cat's tongue
on its last drop of milk.

The rain is here:
The brown field will be green again.
The dry skin will be supple again.
The dead flute shall pipe again.

The rains are here now.
The wind gently stirs me up.
It is time to inhale.

This rain, this gift,
latches on my heart's tender leaves.

NGOZI OBASI AWA